SPEEDWAY'S CLASSIC MEETINGS

SPEEDWAY'S CLASSIC MEETINGS

Norman Jacobs & Chris Broadbent

TEMPUS

To Phil and all the members of The British Speedway Forum
www.speedway-forum.co.uk

First published 2005

Tempus Publishing Limited
The Mill, Brimscombe Port,
Stroud, Gloucestershire, GL5 2QG
www.tempus-publishing.com

British Library Cataloguing in Publication Data.
A catalogue record for this book is available from the British Library.

ISBN 0 7524 3554 X

Typesetting and origination by Tempus Publishing Limited.
Printed in Great Britain.

Contents

Introduction and Acknowledgements

Speedway was born in this country on 19 February 1928. Since then there have been literally thousands of meetings up and down the length and breadth of the country. The vast majority have provided a great afternoon or evening's entertainment and have given the fans something to talk about to while away the hours until the following week's meeting. Once every now and then, however, a meeting comes along that will be talked about not just until the next meeting takes place but remain in the memory forever. These are the classic meetings.

There can be many reasons why a meeting becomes a classic. It can be because it was the first of its kind, because there was an unexpected performance by an underdog, because of an amazing comeback, because of a last-heat decider that settled the outcome of a major trophy, because of a controversial episode, because the racing throughout the match was full of incident with passing and repassing in every heat. All of these and more will be found in this book.

Speedway is one of the few sports that is equally enjoyable in individual, team or other formats and we have tried to reflect this variety in the meetings chosen. It is also a sport where the fans, perhaps more so than those of any other sport, place value on the quality and closeness of the racing rather than the level of the participants, and we have included meetings of all standards to reflect this too, from World Championship finals to Second Division qualifying rounds; from World Team Cup finals to Second Division league matches.

There are a number of people we would like to thank for helping make this book possible, either by setting aside time to talk to us about their memories or by lending us photographs and other material. These include Ron Johnston, John Louis, Malcolm Simmons, Peter Williams, Stan Stevens, Ian Hoskins, Reg Trott, Roy Craighead, Ian Cartwright, Terry Stone, Bob Andrews, Tommy Sweetman, Len Read, John Chaplin, Dave Lanning, the Farndon family, Dick Barrie, Dennis Wallace, Ian Moultray, Mike Kemp, Paul Tadman, Chris Fenn, Ken Wrench, Alison Copland, Ian Corcoran, John and Margaret Broadbent, Martyn Cornwell, Brian Longman, Steve Hone, Paul Scott, Carl Nicklin, Kevin Leakey, Doug MacFarlane, Keith Hulme, Ghillean Bates-Salter, John Somerville, Phil Hood, Ken Beattie, Ken Wrench, Allan Morrey, Chris Young, Steve Dixon, Mike Hunter, Ken Taylor, Bryan Tungate, John Hill, Trevor James, Janet Hambleton, Graham Fraser and Jim Henry of *Speedway Researcher* and Nick Barber. We would also like to thank members of the Internet British Speedway Forum for their support and suggestions as to which meetings might be included in this book.

The front cover photograph is copyright of Mike Patrick and reproduced by kind permission. The illustrations on pages 30 and 32 are from the John Chaplin collection and reproduced by kind permission. The illustrations on pages 62 and 88-93 are reproduced by kind permission of F.O.E.S. Photographic Archive.

19 February 1928, High Beech

The First Meeting in Britain

It would be impossible to start a book on Classic Meetings with anything other than the first recognised speedway meeting in Great Britain, which took place at High Beech on 19 February 1928. Speedway was already well established in Australia and to some extent America before it was exported to Great Britain. The fact it arrived over here when it did was largely due to Lionel Wills, a motorcycling undergraduate at Cambridge. He first saw speedway in 1926 while on a visit to Australia. After having a go at it himself he wrote home to the motorcycling press in this country, describing what he had seen together with his own experience, and urged motorcycle clubs to take up this new sport.

It was Jack Hill-Bailey, honorary secretary of the Ilford Motor Cycle and Light Car Club, who was quickest off the mark and, following discussions with Wills on his return and an Australian rider, Keith McKay, who arrived in England in October 1927, he organised the now-famous High Beech meeting. The site eventually chosen was a disused cycle track behind the King's Oak public house in the heart of Epping Forest in Essex. After a false start, when he attempted to stage the meeting on 9 November 1927 but was refused a licence by the Auto Cycle Union (ACU), the meeting finally took place on 19 February 1928.

Mr and Mrs Hill-Bailey set out for High Beech from their Ilford home on a bright crisp morning, armed with 2,000 admission tickets and 500 programmes, hoping they might just sell out. The meeting was due to start at 10.30 a.m. By the time the Hill-Baileys arrived at 8 a.m. there were already 2,000 people waiting to get in. By the start time, an estimated crowd of between 12,000 and 15,000 had arrived with more still pouring in, causing traffic jams on all roads between Epping and London. The final estimated number of people turning up was placed at between 20,000 and 30,000. Considering the meeting had had very scant advertising this was a remarkable turnout. There had been five lines in *The Motor Cycle* and just a few words in the Club Notes column of *Motor Cycling*.

Part of the ACU's conditions for allowing the meeting was that spectators had to view the racing from the centre green behind a rope barrier. It soon became obvious that this was impossible. Thousands of spectators were swarming all round the track, some even taking up vantage points in the trees that overlooked the venue.

Forty-two riders were down to compete in the day's racing in eight main events, consisting of over fifty races with heats, semi-finals and finals. There was no such thing as a purpose-built speedway bike, of course, and the riders, who were mostly road racers or trials riders, turned up on their own bikes, stripping them down just prior to the commencement of racing. In fact, some did not even do that and rode with their lamps, horns and speedometers still in place. Unfortunately, the very first race of the

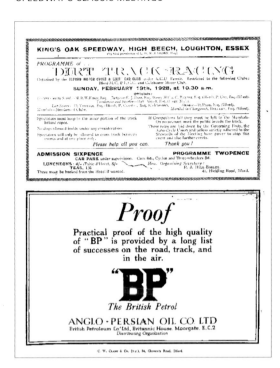

Left: Programme cover.

Below: The crowd was so big at the first meeting that many had to climb nearby trees to see the racing.

Opposite: The start of the Ilford Novices' Event, the first final at the first meeting. From left to right: Ivor Creek, Fred Ralph, Hugh Smythe, Sonny Wilson. The race was won by Fred Ralph.

first speedway meeting in this country, round one of the Ilford Novice Event, proved to be an anti-climax as there was only one competitor. His name was Mr A. Barker and he tootled round sedately on his Ariel, more concerned with not falling off than giving a demonstration of racing.

The first semi-final saw Fred Ralph, mounted on a 344cc Coventry Eagle, up against Ivor Creek on his 490cc Norton. It was a close race but Ralph just managed to hold off Creek for the victory. The second semi-final came down to a race between Hugh Smyth on his 493cc ohv Sunbeam and Sonny Wilson on his much smaller 172cc Francis-Barnett. Amazingly, Wilson managed to keep pace with Smyth but was just beaten on the line.

The first final of the day proved to be the most exciting race so far as, for two laps, Creek, Smyth and Ralph raced neck and neck. As they entered the third lap Creek found some extra speed and raced off into the lead but, on the fifth and final lap (all races that day were due to be held over five laps), he skidded wildly and Ralph was able to ride round the outside and take the first speedway title to be raced for in Great Britain, the Ilford Novices Event.

As none of the riders concerned in these races had actually seen any real speedway they were not sure what they were supposed to do. In fact, not only did none of them broadside, they even held it to be unethical to put their foot down on the track while racing and their feet remained glued to the footrests throughout the race. In any case, the ACU had ruled that the bikes must have rear brakes fitted. These brakes were used often and sometimes violently as the riders tried valiantly to get to grips with this new form of racing.

There were, however, two Australians among the competitors: Keith McKay, who had helped arrange the meeting, and Billy Galloway, the 'Demon Barber', who had arrived in this country just before Christmas 1927. Hill-Bailey was hoping that these two would show the British crowd how real speedway was raced. First Australian out was Galloway, who took on one of Britain's leading motorcycle exponents, Colin Watson, among others, in heat three of the second event, the Five Lap Solo Machine Event. Galloway got off to a bad start as his engine briefly cut out entering the second bend, causing him to drop back to last place. Getting over his temporary problem, he opened the throttle full out and swept into the third bend but, instead of broadsiding, he went in to a series of spectacular skids. Eventually his greater experience told and he passed the others, catching and passing Watson on the last lap to take the chequered flag. However, much to Hill-Bailey's disappointment, even Galloway had managed to win without once putting his foot down. He explained afterwards that the surface was unsuitable for sliding. He had been used to continuous loose surfaces on Australian dirt tracks but High Beech was a hard cinder track. Galloway was also riding under another big handicap in that he was unable to use his own bike and instead had to borrow Freddie Dixon's Isle of Man TT machine with road racing gearing. Even worse for Galloway was the fact that he never managed to get out of bottom gear because, as he said afterwards, he didn't know how to.

Heat seven of event two saw one of the most exciting races of the day as local Essex-born Alf Medcalf took on C.M. Harley and Jack Barrett. Medcalf took an early lead with Harley in hot pursuit. Barrett got a poor start but chased after the others at full speed, eventually catching and passing Harley on the third lap. Still roaring round the track he caught up Medcalf and the two of them raced on side by side, careering into the bends, neither giving an inch. For over half a lap they hurtled round as if locked together and then the inevitable happened. Their machines touched and both went down, leaving Harley to finish the race alone.

The second semi-final was another fine race as Harley and Reg Pointer got out of the start together and stayed together for the first two laps. Behind them, McKay, who had not made a good start, was gradually inching his way towards them and, by superior cornering, finally caught them. Having passed Harley he drew level with Pointer and the two of them lapped side by side. At last, on the final lap, with the crowd cheering wildly, McKay slipped past, just holding his lead by inches over the finishing line.

The final of event two saw the two Australians, McKay and Galloway, up against two British riders, Pointer and Alf Foulds. Although the race was expected to go to the two experienced Aussies it was, in fact, the British rider, Alf Foulds, who took the lead with Pointer behind him. Galloway in third place was pressing Pointer hard when suddenly, on lap three, he fell. In trying to avoid the fallen Galloway, McKay pulled an evasive skid and managed to lose his tyre, leaving the two English riders, Foulds and Pointer, to come in first and second as the only two finishers. This is, incidentally, the first known example of an English rider beating an Australian.

Event three was a sidecar event and was won by C.M. Harley. This was followed by a long lunch break as the spectators took themselves off to the nearby towns of Epping

Right: The Australian, Billy Galloway, falls in the second final, the Solo Machines Event, while trying to pass Reg Pointer. Keith McKay can just be seen behind.

Below: Alf Foulds, winner of event two for solo machines, went on to become a leading rider with Lea Bridge.

and Loughton for refreshments. All the morning events had been over the designated five laps but, owing to lack of time, the afternoon's events were cut to three. The first event after lunch was event four, the Three Laps Novices Event. After seeing the Australians and the top British riders out earlier this proved to be a little slow and tame for the crowds, though there was a spectacular crash in the second heat as L.J. Poole and W.W. Cockburn both hit a deep rut caused by the sidecars and were thrown from their bikes. Luckily neither was hurt. The final of this event was won by G. Fletcher from Ivor Creek with Arnold Day in third place.

The semi-final of event five, the Three Laps Solo Machines Event, saw another exciting race as Pointer jumped into the lead followed closely by Medcalf. By now the best of the British boys had begun to learn how to skid a little round the bends and, with these two being two of the best, an enthralling contest took place as they tried to outskid each other. Eventually, on the last lap, Medcalf managed to slip past Pointer to win the race. Reg Pointer, however, had his revenge in the final as he led from start to finish, winning in grand style.

Event six was for sidecars and was won by Arthur Noterman who beat Alf Foulds into second place. The next event to be run (event seven having been cancelled owing to lack of time) was a series of attempts by various riders on the 'Fastest Lap from Standing Start' record and was won by Alf Medcalf, who recorded a time of 26.8 seconds, beating Alf Foulds (27.0) and Reg Pointer (27.2). This was a little surprising as both Foulds and Pointer were racing 500cc machines – Foulds a 493cc Sunbeam and Pointer a 497cc Ariel – whereas Medcalf was mounted on a much smaller 348cc Douglas. The final event was a similar one for sidecars and was won by Arthur Noterman in a time of 30.0.

Despite the fact that spectators were all over the place, inside and outside the track, there were no safety fences and, in spite of the fact there were numerous falls as the riders tried to get to grips with this new type of racing, the day passed off with no-one getting injured. The most serious casualty was when one of the riders, Dicky Bird, managed to swallow a wasp while racing.

A number of the leading riders on that historic day went on to become early stars of the sport, including Alf Medcalf, who was signed up by International Speedways and featured at the opening meetings of their tracks at White City, Wimbledon and Harringay; Fred Ralph, who became a member of the Stamford Bridge team that won the very first league championship; Ivor Creek, one of West Ham's first stars; Reg Pointer, who became a popular rider at Wimbledon and White City; Alf Foulds, who was a hero at Lea Bridge and, perhaps the best of the lot, Colin Watson, who later went on to become an England Test star and captain of Wembley. There were also a number of other riders who did not take part on that opening day but were present among the crowd. These included Wal Philips, another Test star and member of the same Stamford Bridge team as Fred Ralph, and Ginger Lees, later of Preston and Wembley, who was to set a record individual score of 22 points in a Test match against Australia in 1933. It was Lees who is said to have originated the foot-forward method of riding.

There can be no doubt at all that the meeting at High Beech had been an unqualified success, far exceeding the expectations of its organisers and laying the foundations for the sport of speedway in this country. Jack Hill-Bailey's summary of the day may be one of the greatest understatements of all time when he said: 'It looks as though we have started something.'

In his official report of the meeting, Hill-Bailey said: 'My committee and I had decided that if 3,000 people turned up we should have done well… It so happened, however, that 19 February was a beautiful day and the result was that, an hour before the start of the meeting, all tickets had been sold, every programme had gone, the entrance gate had been pushed over and all hope of collecting any further money had vanished! The governing body had insisted that all spectators were to be kept behind the rope barrier inside the track. It soon became obvious that there was little chance of anyone observing this rule and, in fact, the racing was actually carried out between two closely packed lines of spectators. Frankly the whole meeting was a nightmare for every one of the officials. We expected every moment to see some daring rider lose control of his machine and crash into the crowd, but there was no such accident.'

Billy Galloway, remembering the meeting many years later, said: 'I did a great deal of racing in my time starting in West Maitland and graduating to England, Scotland,

Of all the riders present at the first meeting at High Beech, Colin Watson went on to have the most success. Here he is featured on the front cover of *Speedway News* two years later in 1930.

Egypt and France but my most memorable and frightening experience was at the High Beech opening when thousands more spectators turned up than was expected. They stormed onto the grass inside the track that was marked off only with white paint and possessed no safety fence, while people climbed trees on the outside, some falling on the track. When the competitors tried to ride the white line, onlookers couldn't move back so they literally had to draw in their stomachs!'

In spite of the excitement and its importance to speedway, there was one man present at the meeting who was not too impressed with the day's proceedings and that was the Australian promoter A.J. Hunting. Johnnie Hoskins notwithstanding, Mr Hunting had become the leading promoter of speedway in the world and had under his wing most of the leading Aussies of the time including Frank Arthur and Vic Huxley. He sought out Hill-Bailey after the meeting and simply said: 'My boy, you're all wrong – this isn't the way to run a dirt-track meeting.'

Whether it was or it wasn't, the new craze spread like wildfire and, to use a well-worn cliché, the rest, as they say, is history.

High Beech, 19 February 1928

Results of Finals

Event One – Ilford Novices (Five laps)
1   Fred Ralph (344cc Coventry-Eagle)
2   Ivor Creek (490cc Norton)
3   Hugh Smyth (493cc Sunbeam)
Winner's Time: 2m 10s

Event Two – Solo Machines (Five laps)
1   Alf Foulds (493cc Sunbeam)
2   Reg Pointer (497cc Ariel)
Billy Galloway and Keith McKay did not finish
Winner's Time: 2m 2s

Event Three – Sidecars (Five Laps)
1   C.M. Harley (488cc Zenith)
Winner's Time: 2m 29s

Event Four – Novices (Three laps)
1   G. Fletcher (557cc Ariel)
2   Ivor Creek (490cc Norton)
3   Arnold Day (493cc Sunbeam)
Winner's Time: 1m 25s

Event Five – Solo Machines (Three laps)

1   Reg Pointer (497cc Ariel)
2   A. Duce (349cc AJS)
3   P.R. Bradbrook (344cc Coventry-Eagle)

Winner's Time: 1m 17s

Event Six – Sidecars (Three laps)

1   Arthur Noterman (498cc Triumph)
2   Alf Foulds (493cc Sunbeam)
3   H. Lock (498cc AJS)

Winner's Time: 1m 23.2s

Event Seven – Cancelled owing to lack of time

Event Eight – One Lap Standing Start Record Attempt

Solo Machines

1   Alf Medcalf (348cc Douglas) 26.8s
2   Alf Foulds (493cc Sunbeam) 27.0s
3   Reg Pointer (497cc Ariel) 27.2s

Sidecars

1   Arthur Noterman (498cc Triumph) 30.0s
2   L.J. Pellat (344cc OK Supreme) 30.6s
3   Alf Foulds (493cc Sunbeam) 31.6s

28 July 1928, Belle Vue (Kirkmanshulme Lane)

The First Meeting at Belle Vue

Ever since the first meeting held at Belle Vue, Manchester, on 28 July 1928, the name Belle Vue has become synonymous with speedway in this country. It is the only club to have staged league racing every year since the introduction of league racing in 1929 and is the only club to have put on speedway every year since 1928, including the Second World War years.

Although Belle Vue can claim this pre-eminence in the speedway world it did not, in fact, hold the first speedway meeting in Manchester. Notwithstanding the fact that High Beech has come to be recognised as the first speedway meeting in this country there are those who would argue that it was beaten to it by a dirt track meeting held in a venue known as Moorside Stadium on Dodd's Farm in Droylsden on 25 June 1927. This meeting was organized by Harrison Gill of the South Manchester Motor Club on a narrow 440-yard circuit. Cinders for the track were supplied by the nearby East Manchester Corporation Power Station. These were packed down hard on the surface leaving no loose cinders to enable any sliding to take place. Eight hundred spectators attended. The first race was won by a local motorcycle dealer, Fred Fearnley, and the winner of the 'Experts' Race' was Charlie Pashley. The most successful rider of the day was Ron Caves, who managed to win two events. Nothing happened after this meeting, however, and it wasn't until the High Beech meeting that interest in speedway took off and tracks began to spring up all over the country, not least in Manchester.

Two more tracks were to open before Belle Vue made its first appearance: Audenshaw on 3 March 1928 and White City on 16 June 1928. The Audenshaw meeting was also organized by the South Manchester Motor Club and was heavily advertised beforehand by the two Australians who had appeared at High Beech, Keith McKay and Billy Galloway. Among those taking part at Manchester's first proper speedway meeting were Alec Jackson, Ginger Lees, Bob Harrison and Acorn Dobson. McKay and Galloway took part in a special exhibition race between the top local riders and the two Australians. The race was won by McKay after Galloway suffered engine failure.

The White City track measured a quarter of a mile and was run by the British Dirt Track Racing Association, who had managed to book in one of the sport's top stars for the opening meeting in American Sprouts Elder who, not surprisingly, won the afternoon's top prize, the Golden Helmet. One local man who impressed was Arthur Franklyn.

The scene was now set for Belle Vue to enter the fray. Because the name Belle Vue belongs to a club rather than a particular track, the famous Aces have raced at two different venues, Kirkmanshulme Lane and Hyde Road, and it was Kirkmanshulme Lane on the site of Belle Vue Greyhound Stadium, opened in 1926 as the first greyhound stadium in the country, which was first off the mark. The opening meeting was organised by International Speedways Ltd under their dynamic managing director,

SPEED NEWS

PROGRAMME
at
MANCHESTER SPEEDWAY
28th July, 1928

Prize Money £160

The Management reserve the right to alter or vary this programme without notice.

OFFICIALS
Manchester

Chief Clerk of Course:
Frank A. Hunting, Esq.

Clerk of Course:
R. S. Maybrook, Esq.

Assistant Clerk of Course:
E. O. Spence.

Medical Officer:

A.C.U. Steward:
W. G. Gabriel, Esq.

Judge—A. S. Morgan.
Timekeeper—H. S. Wheeldon.
Assist. Timekeeper—J. Dearnley.
Starter—E. Campbell.
Lap Scorer—A. Walker.
Telephone Steward—W. Thompson.
Pit Steward—F. Hunt.
Colour Steward—E. N. Bloor.

EVENT 1   To start 2.45 p.m.
GRAND PARADE
AND OPENING OF TRACK.

EVENT 2   To start 3.0 p.m.
MANCHESTER HANDICAP
HEAT 1

Rider	Colour	Hdcp.
Charlie Spinks (A)	Red	2 s.
Jim Kempster (E)	White	2 s.
Mart Seiffert (E)	Blue	2 s.
A. Hill (E)	Yellow	5 s.
L. Hickson (E)	Pink	8 s.
T. Ashburn (E)	Green	9 s.

1st.................. 2nd....................

Time.....................

1st and 2nd transferred to Event 6.

EVENT 3   To start 3.8 p.m.
MANCHESTER HANDICAP
HEAT 2

Rider	Colour	Hdcp.
Frank Arthur (A)	Red	Scr.
Eric Spencer (E)	White	2 s.
Bert Perrigo (E)	Blue	3 s.
A. Ward (E)	Yellow	7 s.
R. Sadebottom (E)	Pink	8 s.
E. Kingdom (E)	Green	9 s.

1st.................. 2nd....................

Time.....................

1st and 2nd transferred to Event 6.

EVENT 4   To start 3.16 p.m.
MANCHESTER HANDICAP.
HEAT 3

Rider	Colour	Handicap
Frank Pearce (A)	Red	2 s.
Jack Parker (E)	White	2 s.
O. Langton (E)	Blue	5 s.
F. Dobson (E)	Yellow	7 s.
S. Allen (E)	Pink	8 s.
J. Boulton (E)	Green	9 s.

1st.................. 2nd....................

Time.....................

1st and 2nd transferred to Event 7.

EVENT 5   To start 3.24 p.m.
MANCHESTER HANDICAP.
HEAT 4

Rider	Colour	Handicap
Vic Huxley (A)	Red	Scr.
Noel Johnson (A)	White	2 s.
E. Langton (E)	Blue	5 s.
A. Jackson (E)	Yellow	5 s.
E. Flinn (E)	Pink	7 s.
C. Manson (E)	Green	9 s.

1st.................. 2nd....................

Time.....................

1st and 2nd transferred to Event 7.

EVENT 6   To start 3.42 p.m.
HANDICAP
1ST SEMI-FINAL.

No.	Rider	Colour	Hdcp.
1		Red	
2		White	
3		Blue	
4		Yellow	

1st.................. 2nd....................

Time.....................

1st and 2nd transferred to Event 17.

EVENT 7   To start 3.50 p.m.
HANDICAP
2ND SEMI-FINAL

No.	Rider	Colour	Hdcp.
1		Red	
2		White	
3		Blue	
4		Yellow	

1st.................. 2nd....................

Time.....................

1st and 2nd transferred to Event 17

EVENT 8   To start 3.58 p.m.
GOLD HELMET
HEAT 1

Rider	Colour
Charlie Spinks (A)	Red
Eric Spencer (E)	White
Bert Perrigo (E)	Blue
A. Ward (E)	Yellow

1st.................. Time....................

1st transferred to Event 15.

Programme cover.

The (Manchester) *Evening Chronicle's* cartoonist's view of the racing at Belle Vue and Manchester White City on 28 July 1928.

Mr A.J. Hunting. Hunting had a comparatively long history of promoting the sport in Australia and, when speedway tracks began to open in Great Britain, Hunting and his company were there to make sure they had a large slice of the action. He had arrived earlier in the year with most of the established stars of Australian speedway already under contract to him, including Vic Huxley, Frank Arthur, Hilary Buchanan and Ben Unwin, and set about building new tracks. His first to open was at London White City on 19 May 1928, followed in quick succession by Wimbledon, Harringay and Hall Green, Birmingham, and then on 28 July by Kirkmanshulme Lane.

The meeting was preceded by a special luncheon held at the Midland Hotel hosted by Mr Arthur Johnson, one of the directors of International Speedways Ltd. At this lunch it was announced that the famous motor racing driver and holder of the world land speed record, Major Henry Segrave, had been appointed technical motorist for International Speedways.

As befitted the occasion, the new track was due to be opened with all due ceremony by one of Britain's leading airmen, the Master of Sempill. Earlier in the day a telegram was received by the organisers stating that he was just about to leave London for Manchester. However, by the appointed start time of 3 p.m. there was no sign of the Master of Sempill, so the meeting went ahead without him.

Those taking part were a mixture of Hunting's contracted Australian riders, including Frank Arthur, Vic Huxley and Charlie Spinks, some of the leading English riders now contracted to International Speedway tracks, such as Jack Parker, Jim Kempster and Mart Sieffert, and a number of local lads trying their hand at this new-fangled sport including Eric and Oliver Langton and Alec Jackson, all of whom were later to make a name for themselves.

Although he did eventually make it, Vic Huxley nearly joined the Master of Sempill on the missing list. He had set off for Manchester by road with his special bike in a trailer, but just as he was leaving London the machine fell off and was smashed. He left the wreckage where it was and dashed back to Charing Cross Station where he had stored his other bike and then sped to Euston Station on his dirt-track machine, minus silencer and gear-box, arriving barely in time to catch the train on which the other Australians were travelling.

'Daredevil' Charlie Spinks, a leading Australian rider with International Speedways Ltd, took part at Belle Vue's first meeting at Kirkmanshulme Lane.

The main event of the afternoon was the race for the Gold Helmet, a trophy valued at £100, which had been met on arrival in Manchester by the police and given an escort to the track.

A crowd of over 15,000 saw Mr William Robbins, a director of International Speedways, standing in for the Master of Sempill, cut the ribbon stretched across the course and declare the track open. The first event was the Manchester Handicap. In the opening heat Charlie Spinks and Jim Kempster rode neck and neck for two laps before Kempster turned on the style to win the race in brilliant fashion. In the second heat, Frank Arthur used all his experience to overcome a two-second handicap and win comfortably from England's Eric Spencer. Heat three saw another easy win, this time by Jack Parker over Frank Dobson. But heat four caused something of a sensation as local boy Alec Jackson put one over on Vic Huxley, beating him into second place. Even though Jackson received a five-second start on Huxley, the famous Australian was still expected to have little difficulty in overcoming the opposition. Perhaps all that racing across London had not done Huxley's bike any good!

The first semi-final pitted the winners and runners-up of heats one and two against each other. Once again Kempster rode an excellent race, this time to hold off the Aussie ace Arthur. In the second semi-final, the crowd got their first taste of how dangerous a sport speedway could be as Parker careered into the back of Huxley. Both were flung with some force from their bikes and men and machines were spread out all along the straight. After a pause for medical attention, and to the relief of everyone present, an announcement was made that neither man was seriously injured and the race would be rerun. Obviously not too shaken by his ordeal, Parker won the race with Jackson following him for second place.

Everything was set for an exciting final with Jim Kempster, Frank Arthur, Jack Parker and Alec Jackson taking their places at the start line. This time the Englishmen could not repeat their success over the lone Australian and Kempster was forced to accept the runner-up spot behind Arthur.

The Gold Helmet was run along similar lines with heats, semi-finals and a final, although this time there was no handicapping. Once again it was Frank Arthur who triumphed, adding the Gold Helmet to his Manchester Handicap Title.

Even though they had brought along some of the top riders in the world, International Speedways had taken a bit of a chance in opening up on 28 July as across town the already established Manchester White City was also holding a meeting, hosting what it said was the first England *v.* Scotland International Speedway Match in history as four riders from Glasgow took on four riders from Manchester. The result of this first international was a 5-5 draw. The principle attraction of the afternoon, however, was the *Sunday Chronicle* Dirt Track Challenge Trophy, won by local rider Arthur Franklyn, who was already beginning to make a name for himself on the northern dirt track circuit. The attendance figure at White City was almost double that at Belle Vue, with 27,000 present.

Altogether thirteen meetings were held at Kirkmanshulme Lane in 1928. It did not open in 1929 and the name Belle Vue Speedway was switched to a new track nearby in Hyde Road, built at the sports ground in Belle Vue Pleasure Gardens. The gardens themselves had opened in 1834 as 'tea gardens', later expanding into prime pleasure gardens with ballrooms, a zoo and a fairground complete with scenic railway. The first motorcycle meetings to take place at the venue were in fact grass track meetings, the first being held as early as 1 October 1927 and then again on 25 February 1928, just six days after the first High Beech meeting, which included a number of future dirt track stars including Eric Langton, Frank Varey, Alec Jackson, Ginger Lees, Acorn Dobson and Dusty Haigh.

The first proper speedway meeting was held on 23 March 1929 under the auspices of the North Manchester Motor Cycle Club. It was advertised as a 'Great Gathering of Stars under the leadership of Arthur Franklyn'. Among those billed to appear were Acorn Dobson, Crazy Hutchins, Hurricane Hatch, Smoke Robinson, Ham Burrill, Bob Harrison, Alec Jackson and Frank Varey. The programme was also to include a 'Demonstration race by Franklyn's Mystery Riders'. Admission was 1*s* (5p), 2*s* (10p) and 3*s* (15p), including free transfer to Belle Vue Gardens.

Twenty-five thousand turned up for the opening meeting to see Arthur Franklyn win the two principle prizes on offer, the Golden Helmet and the *Evening Chronicle* Cup, while George Hazard won the Mancunian Cup. The local paper, the *Evening Chronicle*, was full of praise for Franklyn who, according to their journalist's report of the meeting on 25 March, demonstrated his superiority in no uncertain fashion. The report went on to say: 'I think that no-one can now criticise his style of riding. If at White City last year he was a little inclined to ignore the broadside and play for safety, he showed no desire to do likewise at Belle Vue. His wide broadsiding was just superb. While Hatch and Robinson rode without regard to danger, I think they will need a good deal more practice before they can catch Franklyn.'

Right & Below: A number of local riders also took part in the meeting including Eric Langton and Frank Varey, who went on to become two of England's leading riders in the 1930s.

North Manchester Motor Club

PRESIDENT: J. HENRY ILES, Esq.

PROGRAMME

BELLE VUE SPEEDWAY

Saturday, March 23rd, 1929.

At 7-0 p.m.

The Management reserve the right to alter or vary this Programme without notice.

Held under the General Competition and Special Track Rules of the Auto Cycle Union, together with the Supplementary Regulations of the Club.

Track Licence No. 318.

Prize Money and Appearance Fees in accordance with the Scales authorised by the Northern Dirt Track Owners' Association.

Extract from Supplementary Regulations :—" If, in the opinion of the Clerk-of-the-Course, a fallen rider lies on the Track to the danger of other riders, and by his having fallen, definitely jeopardises the chances of a following competitor, the race will be stopped by the display of the Red Track Lights, and immediately re-run."

OFFICIALS.

CLERK-OF-THE-COURSE - -	E. O. SPENCE, ESQ.
JUDGE - - - -	A. S. MORGAN, ESQ.
STARTER - - - -	J. W. CAMPBELL, ESQ.
TIMEKEEPER - - - -	H. S. WHEELDON, ESQ.
PIT STEWARD - - - -	R. BOYES, ESQ.
MECHANICAL SUPERINTENDENT	M. GAVSON, ESQ.
TREASURER - - - -	S. CHESTER, ESQ.
TRACK MANAGER - - -	B. L. BROOK, ESQ.

Opening Demonstration

Franklyn's Mystery Riders

IN FOUR-LAP RACE.

WHO ARE THEY ?

The programme cover for the first meeting at Hyde Road on 23 March 1929.

For the second week two mouth-watering match races were lined up between Franklyn and Eric Langton and Hurricane Hatch ('second only to Franklyn at Belle Vue') and Ginger Lees. Less than two months later Belle Vue raced their first league match, an English Dirt Track League match against Preston, which they won with some ease 40-21. Among the riders to turn out for Belle Vue in their inaugural league campaign were Frank Varey, Arthur Franklyn, Bob Harrison, Norman Hartley, George Hazard, Riskit Riley and Ian Ritchings. Since that first league encounter Belle Vue have maintained the record of taking part in senior league racing every season; the only club to be able to claim this proud record and it was the Hyde Road track that was to carry the name Belle Vue forward in to speedway pre-eminence for almost the next sixty years until it was sold off for development at the end of the 1987 season.

In 1988 the name Belle Vue switched back to its birthplace at Kirkmanshulme Lane when, on 1 April that year, a new era in the life of the club started with the Frank Varey Northern Trophy, named after the man who had been at the very first Hyde Road meeting and had gone on to become one of England's leading pre-war riders. After retirement he had gone in to management, managing Sheffield for various periods between 1945 and 1972 before returning to Belle Vue as manager in 1974. Belle Vue has remained at Kirkmanshulme Lane ever since.

Our Trophies for Cracks of the Dirt Track.

"Evening Chronicle" cups were competed for by dirt-track riders at Belle Vue and White City on Saturday. Left, A. Franklyn being complimented by Mr. J. H. Iles, president of the North Manchester Motor Club, after winning the trophy at Belle Vue; and left, A. W. Jervis, the successful rider at White City, receiving the cup from Miss Mercedes Gleitze, the famous swimmer.

How the *Evening Chronicle* reported Arthur Franklyn's win at Hyde Road's first meeting.

First Meeting at Belle Vue, Kirkmanshulme Lane, 28 July 1928

Manchester Handicap

Heat 1	Rider	Colour	Handicap	Result	Time
	Charlie Spinks (A)	Red	2s	2nd	–
	Jim Kempster (E)	White	2s	1st	–
	Mart Sieffert (E)	Blue	2s	–	–
	Alec Hill (E)	Yellow	5s	–	–
	L. Hickson (E)	Pink	8s	–	–
	T. Ashburn (E)	Green	9s	–	–

Heat 2	Rider	Colour	Handicap	Result	Time
	Frank Arthur (A)	Red	Scr	1st	–
	Eric Spencer (E)	White	2s	2nd	–
	Bert Perrigo (E)	Blue	3s	–	–
	A. Ward (E)	Yellow	7s	–	–
	R. Sadebottom	Pink	8s	–	–
	E. Kingdom	Green	9s	–	–

Heat 3	Rider	Colour	Handicap	Result	Time
	Frank Pearce (A)	Red	2s	–	–
	Jack Parker (E)	White	2s	1st	–
	Oliver Langton (E)	Blue	5s	–	–
	Frank Dobson (E)	Yellow	7s	2nd	–
	S. Allen (E)	Pink	8s	–	–
	J. Boulton (E)	Green	9s	–	–

Heat 4	Rider	Colour	Handicap	Result	Time
	Vic Huxley (A)	Red	Scr	2nd	–
	Noel Johnson (A)	White	2s	–	–
	Eric Langton (E)	Blue	5s	–	–
	Alec Jackson (E)	Yellow	5s	1st	–
	E. Flinn (E)	Pink	7s	–	–
	C. Manson (E)	Green	9s	–	–

Semi-final 1	Rider	Colour	Handicap	Result	Time
	Jim Kempster (E)	Red	2s	1st	87.5 secs
	Charlie Spinks (A)	White	2s	–	–
	Frank Arthur (A)	Blue	Scratch	2nd	–
	Eric Spencer (E)	Yellow	2s	–	–

Semi-final 2	Rider	Colour	Handicap	Result	Time
	Jack Parker (E)	Red	2s	1st	89.2 secs
	Frank Dobson (E)	White	7s	–	–
	Alec Jackson (E)	Blue	5s	2nd	–
	Vic Huxley (A)	Yellow	Scr	–	–

Final	Rider	Colour	Handicap	Result	Time
	Jim Kempster (E)	Red	2s	2nd	–
	Frank Arthur (A)	White	Scr	1st	–
	Jack Parker (E)	Blue	2s	–	–
	Alec Jackson (E)	Yellow	5s	–	–

Gold Helmet

Heat 1	Rider	Colour	Result	Time
	Charlie Spinks (A)	Red	1st	–
	Eric Spencer (E)	White	2nd	–
	Bert Perrigo (E)	Blue	–	–
	A. Ward (E)	Yellow	–	–

Heat 2	Rider	Colour	Result	Time
	Frank Arthur (A)	Red	1st	82.0 secs
	Jim Kempster (E)	White	2nd	–
	Mart Sieffert (E)	Blue	–	–
	Alec Hill (E)	Yellow	–	–

Heat 3	Rider	Colour	Result	Time
	Frank Pearce (A)	Red	–	–
	Noel Johnson (A)	White	–	–
	Alec Jackson (E)	Blue	–	–
	E. Flinn (E)	Yellow	–	–

Heat 4	Rider	Colour	Result	Time
	Vic Huxley (A)	Red	–	–
	Jack Parker (E)	White	–	–
	Eric Langton (E)	Blue	–	–
	Frank Dobson (E)	Yellow	–	–

Final	Rider	Colour	Result	Time
	Charlie Spinks (A)	Red	–	–
	Frank Arthur (A)	White	1st	–

30 June 1930, Wimbledon

England *v.* Australia: The First Test Match

The highlight of any cricket season has always been its Test match series, particularly the Ashes series between England and Australia. With Australia being the leading speedway nation in the early years of the sport in this country there were a number of attempts to emulate the example of cricket by putting on England *v.* Australia speedway Test matches. For example, Crystal Palace's opening meeting on 19 May 1928 featured a 'Great International Match' for a £100 prize between England and Australia that consisted of just three riders in three heats in the form of three match races between one rider from each side. With Lionel Wills and Roger Frogley of England beating Ron Johnson and Charlie Datson of Australia respectively, the match was won by England by two races to one. The other race ended in a victory for Aussie Sig Schlam over Les Blakebrough.

The following year, 1929, two more internationals were organised at Coventry by the man said to have 'invented' league speedway, Jimmy Baxter, and leading Australian rider Frank Arthur. Like the Crystal Palace meeting, they were determined by a series of two-man match races, though in this case there were four riders and they all met each other once, making sixteen heats in all. In the first meeting England were represented by Jack Parker, Wilmot Evans, Arthur Jervis and Syd Jackson, and Australia by Frank Arthur, Max Grosskreutz, Col Stewart and Billy Lamont. Somewhat surprisingly, given those line-ups, England ran out victors by 9.5 points to 6.5. The half point came from a dead heat between Wilmot Evans and Col Stewart.

The second international was held a few weeks later with Australia this time proving successful. At the end of the season, Arthur and Baxter began to recruit an English team to visit Australia for a return series Down Under, but the ACU were not in favour and the idea had to be abandoned.

Over the winter several moves were made towards inaugurating an official Test match series. Vivian Van Damm, the general manager of International Speedways, held talks with the speedway press as to how best to go about it while the Master of Sempill put the idea to a meeting of the Association of Motor Cycle Track Racing Promoters in London. Although most agreed it was a good idea, the rivalry between the different speedway promoters was such that there was no agreement on who should have the honour of holding the first one.

It was the Wimbledon management who then took matters into their own hands and broke the deadlock by adopting a softly-softly approach. Individual meetings were very common at that time and Wimbledon announced plans for holding an 'all-star' meeting on 30 June 1930. As was common practice they approached the other clubs to ask if they would be prepared to allow their leading riders to take part. This proved to be no problem and so Wembley's Jack Ormston was signed up, as were Crystal

Price 6d.

FIRST SPEEDWAY

TEST MATCH

ENGLAND v AUSTRALIA

Wimbledon, June 30th, 1930

THE AUSTRALIAN TEAM HAS BEEN APPROVED BY THE
AUSTRALIAN AUTHORITIES, WHO RECOGNISE THIS EVENT
AS THE FIRST OFFICIAL SPEEDWAY TEST MATCH

TEAMS

ENGLAND	AUSTRALIA
COLOURS—WHITE	COLOURS—RED
No.	No.
1.—JIM KEMPSTER (Capt.) WIMBLEDON.	1.—VIC HUXLEY (Capt.) HARRINGAY.
4.—ROGER FROGLEY CRYSTAL PALACE.	4.—DICKY CASE WIMBLEDON.
2.—FRANK VAREY MANCHESTER.	2.—FRANK ARTHUR STAMFORD BRIDGE.
5.—WAL PHILLIPS STAMFORD BRIDGE.	5.—RON JOHNSON CRYSTAL PALACE.
3.—JACK PARKER COVENTRY.	3.—MAX GROSSKREUTZ MANCHESTER.
6.—JACK ORMSTON WEMBLEY.	6.—BILLY LAMONT WIMBLEDON.
7.—GUS KUHN STAMFORD BRIDGE. (Res.)	7.—ARNIE HANSEN SOUTHAMPTON (Res.)

The management reserve the right to alter or vary this programme without notice.
The Gramophone Records played at this Track are supplied by the courtesy of The Decca Co.
Meeting Conducted by International Speedways Ltd., 80, Fleet Street, E.C.4.

Programme cover.

Palace's Roger Frogley, Coventry's Jack Parker and so on. Once Wimbledon were certain they had got the riders they needed they announced that they were not organising an individual meeting after all, but a Test match between England and Australia. Naturally there were complaints from the other promoters who felt they had been duped but, after lengthy discussions, it was finally agreed by the ACU and the other promoters that Wimbledon could go ahead with the match on condition that this was to be the first in a series and that the other tracks would get their chance to stage a Test match as well.

Mr Maybrook, Wimbledon's clerk of the course, also had the good sense to cable the Australian authorities, asking for their permission for the match to be labelled an official Test match. The Australian control board replied, firstly agreeing to the proposal and secondly expressing the hope that Australia would win.

And so the Test match was officially on, backed by both the British and Australian speedway establishments, though it is a strange fact that both teams were actually chosen by the Wimbledon management rather than by their own powers that be. The trade and national press, both of whom had been crying out for such a series, were quick off the mark, giving their backing to the venture and devoting acres of space to the build up. The day itself had been carefully chosen as there was an Ashes Test match taking place at Lord's that week, so Wimbledon were able to cash in on the

The Australian team line up at the start of the first Test match, From left to right: Billy Lamont, Max Grosskreutz, Ron Johnson, Frank Arthur, Dicky Case, Vic Huxley.

The Australian team begins the pre-match parade with captain Vic Huxley complete with Australian flag in front.

heightened interest in London at that time. Further publicity was organised by distributing artist-drawn posters depicting riders in death-defying manouvres to all major poster sites in and around London, sending sandwich-board men to cricket grounds around the country and by flying huge kites and banners over horse racing meetings. By the day of the meeting, there had been so much publicity that a sell-out crowd was expected and that was exactly what Wimbledon got. South London fell into the grip of one of the worst traffic jams in its history as a two-mile queue of cars and coaches tried to get in to the car park, affecting traffic for miles around. The start had to be held up for over half an hour while they tried to fit everyone in but, in the end, thousands were turned away.

The two teams for this auspicious occasion were: England: Jim Kempster (captain), Wal Phillips, Roger Frogley, Frank Varey, Jack Parker and Jack Ormston with Gus Kuhn as reserve; Australia: Vic Huxley (captain), Dick Case, Frank Arthur, Ron Johnson, Billy Lamont and Max Grosskreutz, with Arnie Hansen as reserve. As befitting such an important occasion there was much pomp and ceremony before the racing actually started. The English team, in their white jerseys with a red lion emblazoned on their backs, and the Australians, in red with a kangaroo on their backs, lined up on the centre green to be introduced individually to the crowd. As each name was mentioned to loud cheers from the spectators, the rider stepped forward and sat on his machine ready for the grand parade that followed. The introduction of the riders and parade is now a normal feature of speedway racing, but at the time was something new and unique to this first Test match.

Vic Huxley, Australia's captain in the first Test match.

The format was to be the same as that for league matches, which was nine heats with each pair meeting once. There was one addition to the rules and that was there would only be two minutes' grace allowed if a rider was experiencing mechanical trouble at the start of a race.

The first heat brought together the two captains. Kempster, who was also the Wimbledon captain, said before the race that he felt this race would be a pointer to the whole contest, arguing that if Huxley could beat him on his own track there would be no holding the Aussies. Kempster won the toss and took positions one and three for England. But it was to no avail, as Huxley shot away from the start and stayed there. Kempster tried his best but he tried too hard and fell off on the first bend of the fourth lap. At exactly the same moment Case's engine failed, leaving Phillips to take second place. Case pushed his bike for nearly a lap to take third place and grab a point. Huxley's time was a new track record, beating Kempster's old one by two-tenths of a second, lowering it from 73.4 secs to 73.2 secs. If Kempster's pre-match views were right, it did not look good for England.

The second heat saw the England pairing of Roger Frogley and Frank Varey out against Frank Arthur and Ron Johnson. Varey made a poor start, was filled up with dirt on the first corner and did not complete the second lap. Arthur and Johnson, on the other hand, both made cracking starts and were able to stick close together with some immaculate team riding. Frogley was never far behind but he could find no way through and it was the Aussie pairing who took first and second places.

The final pairings came out in heat three, with Jack Parker and Jack Ormston for England and Max Grosskreutz and Billy Lamont for Australia. Unfortunately for England, the story was much the same as heat two, with the two Aussies team riding Parker out of the race. Ormston was well behind and came in a very poor fourth.

Things at last started to look up for England in the next heat. Although Arthur took an early lead, Kempster caught him before the end of the first lap and passed him to lead going into the second lap. Arthur tried hard to get back at Kempster but fell at the end of the second lap. Meanwhile, behind them, another battle was taking place as Johnson was holding off Phillips. Phillips was not expected to do very well at Wimbledon as he was a big-track specialist and Plough Lane was one of the smallest tracks in the country. However, he surprised many in this race by doggedly following in Johnson's tyre tracks

Two of the most exciting speedway riders of all time. 'Cyclone' Billy Lamont takes the outside against Vic Huxley at Wimbledon in 1930.

England captain Jim Kempster.

and then putting in a supreme effort on the last bend to take the Aussie and make it a 5-1 for England. The score was now England 9 Australia 15.

In spite of the newly instituted two-minutes rule there was a long delay before the commencement of the next race as Varey was having problems with his motor. His place was eventually taken by England reserve Gus Kuhn. Once the race started it was to prove to be an excellent race as Lamont just managed to hold Frogley's determined efforts to get past him at bay. On the last lap, however, Lamont's engine packed up leaving Frogley to take the chequered flag; Grosskreutz followed him but Lamont was near enough to the finish to be able to coast home third. There was some criticism of Kuhn for not spotting that Lamont was in trouble and trying that bit harder.

Australia's captain and star was out in heat six but, surprisingly, it was Parker who got the drop on him and led him out of the second bend. With Huxley worrying away behind him, Parker lost his concentration and fell on the third bend leaving Huxley and his partner Case to take the heat with no trouble as Ormston offered no serious opposition.

The next race was definitely the best of the evening as Kempster and Phillips took on Lamont and Grosskreutz. Lamont just got his nose ahead at the start but Kempster stayed with him as they screamed round the bends almost locked together. When they passed the yellow flag they were neck and neck. Going into the final bend, Lamont seemed to find just that bit of extra speed and managed to pull away from Kempster, winning the heat by three lengths. Behind them there was an equally close race going on for third spot until Phillips got into a mess entering the first bend on the last lap and came down, with his machine being flung yards from him.

Only two riders finished the eighth heat as Varey slid off on the second corner and Case, who had already fallen and had managed to remount in less than ten seconds, fell again on the second lap, leaving Huxley to lead Frogley home by a fair margin.

Given the dominance of the Australians it somehow seemed appropriate that the ninth and last heat should see both English riders failing to finish and Arthur and Johnson team ride to a final 5-0 victory.

And so the Australian team had emulated what their cricketing colleagues were doing on the other side of London as Australia won the cricket Test match by seven wickets. The final score of 35-17 was a very fair reflection of what had happened that evening. All the Australians had ridden at the top of their form. Huxley in particular was an inspirational captain. Many seasoned speedway spectators present said they had never seen him ride better, which was saying something as he was already reckoned to be the finest speedway rider in the world. *The Motor Cycle* magazine summed up his riding that night: 'Huxley was on absolutely full lock – fighting back and front wheel skids by sheer strength, several times his model laid very nearly flat, but he always wrenched it up again.' Not far behind him was 'the man with a month to live', 'Cyclone' Billy Lamont. He too had probably never ridden better in his life and amazingly even managed to lower Huxley's new track record to 73.0 seconds in that dazzling heat seven. All the other Australians also rode at their best.

The same could not be said for the English riders. Their performance was disappointing. Kempster and Frogley rode as well as could be expected given the strength of the opposition and Phillips did even better than expected, but Parker was a big disappointment while Varey and Ormston scored just 1 point between them and that was a gift when Parker fell in heat six while in the lead.

The second half of the meeting featured a competition called The Big Six in which each side held a series of match races among themselves to find two finalists to decide the individual champion of the night. Australia were first to go with Vic Huxley against Dick Case. It was no surprise that Huxley won, but what was perhaps a little surprising at that stage of the meeting was that Huxley once again broke the track record, smashing Lamont's new time to finish in 72.6 seconds.

In the other two first round Australian matches, Johnson defeated Arthur and Lamont beat Grosskreutz. A three-rider Australian final was then held between the three winners. As expected this turned into a battle between Huxley and Lamont with very little to separate them on the first lap. Unfortunately for the crowd (and himself) Lamont fell on the first bend of the second lap, leaving Huxley with an easy victory over Johnson.

In the English rounds, Kempster beat Frogley by a quarter of a lap, Phillips had an even easier victory over the very much out of form Varey by half a lap, while the third race was never even finished. Parker conked out on the first corner and the race was rerun. This time Ormston took the lead but suddenly slewed round in Parker's path. Parker, with nowhere to go, hit him amidships and then somersaulted over Ormston, who had miraculously managed to keep upright on his bike. Parker damaged his knee and was unable to take part in a second rerun. Ormston decided he had also had enough and did not take his place in the final. The English final therefore was another match race, this time between Kempster and Phillips. Phillips fell, leaving Kempster to face Huxley in the Grand final.

In the end it had come down to the two captains, but there was no way Kempster was going to get anywhere near Huxley in the sort of form he was in that evening and sure enough the final was something of a disappointment as a race, as Huxley led from start to finish, winning by nearly half the straight.

And so the first Test match meeting finished. In spite of the one-sided nature of the encounter, it had been an enormous success and speedway fans could not wait until the two teams met again. To try and even things up a bit it was agreed to change the format and to have eight-man teams meeting over eighteen heats. It was felt this would give England more of a chance as they had more strength in depth than the Australians. This theory proved correct as England went on to win the remaining four Test matches in the 1930 series.

From then on the England v. Australia Tests remained a staple part of the British speedway season until they were finally abandoned at the end of the 1953 season as Australia were no longer able to find a team of sufficient strength. For a number of years after that Australia combined with New Zealand to race England as Australasia, but that too was abandoned in 1961.

30 June 1930, Wimbledon: England v. Australia, First Test Match:

ENGLAND		1	2	3	Total
1	Jim Kempster (Capt.)	0	3	2	5
2	Wal Philips	2	2	F	4
3	Roger Frogley	1	3	2	6
4	Frank Varey	R	F	–	0
5	Jack Parker	1	F	R	1
6	Jack Ormston	0	1	R	1
7	Gus Kuhn (Res.)	0	–	–	0

AUSTRALIA		1	2	3	Total
1	Vic Huxley (Capt.)	3	3	3	9
2	Dick Case	1	2	F	3
3	Frank Arthur	3	F	3	6
4	Ron Johnson	2	1	2	5
5	Billy Lamont	3	1	3	7
6	Max Grosskreutz	2	2	1	5
7	Arnie Hansen (Res.)	–	–	–	–

Heat 1: Huxley, Phillips, Case, Kempster; 73.2 (track record)

Heat 2: Arthur, Johnson, Frogley, Varey (ret.)

Heat 3: Lamont, Grosskreutz, Parker, Ormston

Heat 4: Kempster, Phillips, Johnson, Arthur (f); 73.2 (equals track record)

Heat 5: Frogley, Grosskreutz, Lamont (e/f), Kuhn

Heat 6: Huxley, Case, Ormston, Parker (f)

Heat 7: Lamont, Kempster, Grosskreutz, Phillips (f): 73.0 (track record)

Heat 8: Huxley, Frogley, Varey (f), Case (f)

Heat 9: Arthur, Johnson, Parker (ret.), Ormston (ret.)

The Big Six

Australia

1: Huxley, Case; 72.6 (Track record)

2: Johnson, Arthur

3: Lamont, Grosskreutz

Final: Huxley, Johnson, Lamont (f)

England

1: Kempster, Frogley

2: Phillips, Varey

3 (Rerun twice): Parker (f.ns), Ormston (ns)

Final: Kempster, Phillips (f)

Grand final: Huxley, Kempster

1 August 1934

New Cross *v*. Harringay: London Cup First Round Second Leg and
Vic Huxley *v*. Tom Farndon: British Match Race Championship

Although the main purpose of the evening's entertainment at the Old Kent Road on
1 August 1934 was the second leg of the London Cup first round tie between New
Cross and Harringay, the main interest centred around Vic Huxley's defence of the
British Match Race Championship against local hero Tom Farndon.

There is no doubt that during the early years of the sport in Great Britain, the late
1920s and early 1930s, Vic Huxley was the top man. Winner of the Star Riders'
Championship and three times runner-up as well as being captain and ever-present in
the Australian Test team, he was the rider everyone wanted to beat. When a new
competition was introduced in 1931, the British Match Race Championship, Huxley
was chosen as one of the first two contestants to race for the title. The idea of the
competition was that two riders would be nominated to contest a series of match races
for the title; the best of three at each rider's home track. If it was a tie after this a further
best-of-three decider would be held at a neutral track. Once a champion had been
established, the Speedway Control Board would nominate a challenger (later regu-
larised to on a monthly basis) to challenge for the title.

The other nominated rider for the first championship series was one of the High
Beech pioneers, Wembley and England's Colin Watson. Huxley won the series to
become the first British Match Race Champion and, although he did lose the title in
the meantime, he once again became champion at the beginning of 1934 when he
defeated West Ham's Tiger Stevenson.

His next nominated challenger was New Cross and England's Tom Farndon. New
Cross had only opened at the beginning of the 1934 season under promoter Fred
Mockford. Previously the team had been based at Crystal Palace but rising costs had
forced Mockford to look for a new track. The track he found was a newly constructed
one just off the Old Kent Road in South London. With limited space for construction
it was a fairly small stadium and the shortest track in the country at just 262 yards.
Farndon was a member of the team that moved over. He had been a good rider at
Crystal Palace and on the verge of a breakthrough into greatness. Just before Crystal
Palace's closure, Farndon had won the 1933 Star Riders' Championship, the early
1930s equivalent of the World Championship. His move to New Cross saw him
continue his rise to stardom as he began the year by winning the London Riders'
Championship, the National League Best Pairs Trophy with New Cross captain Ron
Johnson, breaking the New Cross track record during the Second Test match and shat-
tering the Plymouth track record by an incredible two seconds. All this was enough to
earn him the right to challenge Huxley for the British Match Race title. It was a real
case of the old maestro versus the young pretender.

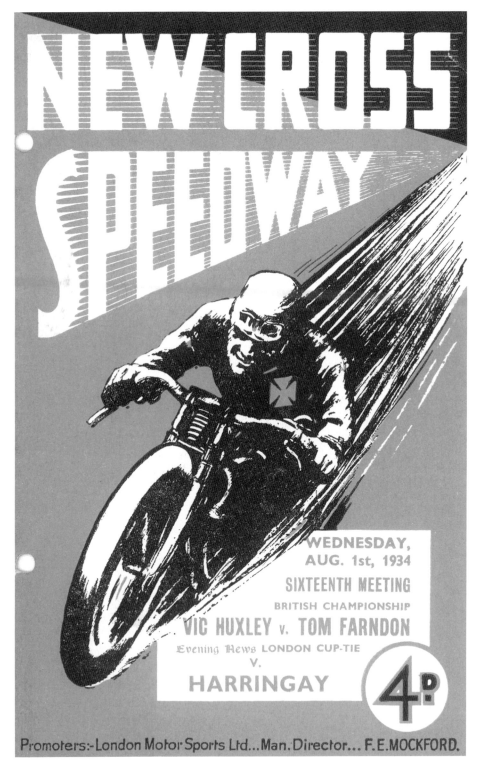

NEW CROSS SPEEDWAY

WEDNESDAY,
AUG. 1st, 1934

SIXTEENTH MEETING

BRITISH CHAMPIONSHIP

VIC HUXLEY v. TOM FARNDON

Evening News LONDON CUP-TIE

v.

HARRINGAY

4D

Promoters:-London Motor Sports Ltd...Man. Director... F.E.MOCKFORD.

Programme cover.

The Tom Webster cartoon that appeared in the *Daily Mail* on 2 August 1934 and that the New Cross promoter, Fred Mockford, felt went 'a long way to establishing speedway racing as a truly national sport'.

Certainly in some sections of the national press, Huxley was seen as the favourite to retain his title. But this did not impress Farndon's promoter, Fred Mockford, who wrote in the New Cross programme: 'I was very annoyed the other day in reading Trevor Wignall's sports article in the *Daily Express*. He was talking about the British Individual Championship and finished up by saying that all the betting is in favour of Vic Huxley. Quite frankly, it seems almost incredible to me that a gentleman of his repute, writing in a leading London newspaper, should insult the intelligence of his readers with such utter piffle. Surely to goodness he should be familiar with what he is writing about, and I can assure you that I, or any other promoter, would be only too pleased to give him all the information that he would require on speedway matters.'

The first leg was held at Huxley's track, Wimbledon, on 30 July. Farndon won the toss and took the inside in the first race. He proved to be much too fast for Huxley as he shot away from the start and never looked likely to be beaten. In beating Huxley

Tom Farndon at the height of his fame.

in the first leg he also took away his track record, lowering it by three-fifths of a second to 69.8. In the second leg, Huxley managed to keep up with Farndon as far as the first corner but Farndon, on the outside this time, went round Huxley as if he was standing still. Once again his time was 69.8. It was obvious a new megastar had arrived on the scene. Anyone who could beat the great Vic Huxley so easily and so convincingly on his own track must surely be the new star of the sport.

The return leg at New Cross was to see an even more sensational development in the rise of the new marvel. As news spread around South London of Farndon's performance at Wimbledon, crowds flocked to the Old Kent Road to see the sport's latest phenomenon and it was in front of a capacity crowd that Huxley won the toss and elected to take the inside position. This time it was Huxley who got away first and for almost two laps the Australian ace kept the youngster at bay, but Farndon was not to be denied and, going round the fourth bend of the second lap, pulled out all the stops and rode a magnificent corner right round the boards, passing Huxley as they came into the home straight. From then on he gradually pulled away, winning the race by eight lengths. Although this had been an exciting enough race in itself, which had brought the crowd to their feet, it was when the time was announced that there were loud gasps from the spectators. The time was 59.6 seconds, smashing the current record, held by Eric Langton, by an astonishing 1.4 seconds. It was also the first time on any track in the country that the magic one-minute mark had been beaten. The second leg was something of an anti-climax as Farndon led from start to finish, winning in 60.2 seconds.

A composite card with various pictures of Vic Huxley signed by the great man himself.

In the following week's programme, Mr Mockford had this to say: 'Congratulations, Tom, on a wonderful performance… I personally feel particularly proud of Tom's accomplishments. I suppose most of you, like myself, were tickled to death when you opened your *Daily Mail* on Thursday morning last and found Mr Tom Webster's cartoon in respect of New Cross Speedway and Tom Farndon. Apart from being a great compliment to us, it is undoubtedly one of the best things in the way of publicity that has appeared in connection with the sport of speedway racing, and I feel that this cartoon has gone a long way to establishing speedway racing as a truly national sport.'

Farndon had beaten the old champion in four straight runs, on every occasion beating the old track record. He was now British Match Race Champion and the only rider ever to hold the Star Riders' Championship, the London Riders' Championship and the British Match Race title simultaneously. In some ways it represented a symbolic change for British speedway as the old Australian master, the man who had dominated the early years of the sport in this country, was beaten by this young up-and-coming English rider. Later that year he saw off two challengers for his title in the shape of his own team captain, Ron Johnson, and Belle Vue's Max Grosskreutz – both Australians. In one of the races against Grosskreutz, Farndon rode what many at the time thought was the best race anyone had ever ridden. Ron Johnson described it as the most thrilling race he had ever seen. Recalling it many years later he said: 'Max was in the middle of the last corner when Tom entered it. He drove his motor 'flat' into and around the bend without moving an inch from the white line and won by half a wheel. I shouted myself hoarse from a seat in the grandstand. I have never seen any rider, before or since, handle a machine like Tom did that night.'

In 1935 he again defeated Max Grosskreutz as well as Hackney's Dick Case, setting up new track records at Hackney and Wembley in the process. Twenty-four coachloads of New Cross supporters travelled to Wembley to see Farndon defeat Case. It seemed that the whole of the speedway world was now at Farndon's feet and that he was certain to become the greatest rider the sport had ever seen. Tragically, it was not to be. Just over a year after becoming champion, Tom Farndon was dead, killed in a crash on the New Cross track in a meaningless second-half event on 28 August 1935.

Following his match race victory, Farndon took his place in the New Cross line-up for the London Cup match against Harringay. The first leg had been held on 14 July and had resulted in a win for New Cross by 63 points to 44, so Harringay had a deficit of 19 to make up if they were to progress to the semi-final.

The first heat saw the New Cross captain Ron Johnson and his partner, Nobby Key, up against the outstanding Harringay pairing of the Parker brothers, Jack and Norman. It was an immediate sign of things to come as Johnson and Key took a reasonably easy 5–1 in the opening heat. The second heat saw another 5–1 to New Cross with Farndon team-riding his partner, Stan Greatrex, home to victory over Phil Bishop and Norman Evans. The next four heats went 4–2, 5–1, 5–1, 4–2, but Harringay managed to stop the rot in heat seven when the Parkers turned in a 5–1 over Joe Francis and George Newton. It was back to normal service in the next two heats as New Cross scored a 5–1 and a 4–2 to put them 22 points ahead on the night and 41 points overall. The

New Cross captain Ron Johnson.

match was turning into a rout. But it was once again the Parker brothers who came to Harringay's rescue as, in heat ten, they took on a so-far unbeaten Ron Johnson and Nobby Key. This time it was Norman who got away in front of Johnson and held on to his lead while behind him Jack was doing the same with Nobby Key. It was a 4–2 to Harringay, making the score 40–20 on the night. Heat eleven reverted to type as New Cross took a 5–1 but, in the following heat, Harringay provided their third winner of the night as Charlie Blacklock defeated the New Cross paring of Joe Francis and George Newton to hold the scores steady with a 3–3.

Heat thirteen was to prove the heat of the night as Harringay's most successful pairing, Jack and Norman Parker, came up against Farndon and Greatrex. The Farndon–Greatrex pairing had so far scored three 5–1s and one 4–2 with Farndon, continuing in the form he had shown in the match races, unbeaten by an opponent. In spite of this, however, it was Norman who was first out of the gate, followed closely by Farndon. Behind, Jack was holding out in front of Greatrex. On the second lap, the race for first place looked all over as Farndon saw his opportunity and passed the younger Parker brother, but Norman would not admit defeat and followed closely, not allowing any further gap to develop. Going into the first bend on the last lap, Parker wrenched his machine to the inside and managed to pull off the unthinkable, as he got through the tiniest of gaps to pass Farndon. The two bikes screamed down the back straight almost together and in to the final bend, but Parker held his position perfectly and denied Farndon victory by the smallest of margins. It had been a truly great race and one of the rare defeats for Farndon. Behind them, Jack had stayed in front of Greatrex, so it was another 4–2 for the Parker brothers, taking the scores on the night to 50–28.

A 3–3 in the following heat was followed by a 3–2 in heat fifteen as Johnson beat Cliff Parkinson with neither of the other two riders finishing. With the two Parkers out in heat sixteen against New Cross's weakest pairing of Francis and Newton, there was some optimism in the Harringay camp that they might close the gap a bit and make the scores a bit more respectable. But it seemed that the sensational heat thirteen had taken it out of Jack and Norman as they trailed in third and fourth.

There was still one twist to come as, in the penultimate heat, Bishop, having failed to score a single point in his first four outings, led from start to finish, followed closely by his partner, Norman Evans, leaving Johnson and Key floundering in third and fourth places to give Harringay their second 5–1 of the night.

Heat eighteen saw Farndon and Greatrex out for New Cross up against Parkinson and Blacklock for Harringay. But this time there was no mistake for Farndon as he roared off from the gate, pulling further and further ahead as the race went on. With Greatrex taking third place it was a 4–2 to New Cross and a convincing victory on the night by 66 points to 41 and an overall victory by 129 to 85.

Only the Parkers and Charlie Blacklock had put up much resistance to the New Cross steamroller. Blacklock in particular had had an exceptionally good night, being Harringay's top scorer with 11 points. Not noted normally as a star performer – his average that year was only 3.3 – he nevertheless rose to the challenge. Like Farndon,

Norman Parker rode the race of his life to beat Tom Farndon in heat thirteen of the London Cup match.

Blacklock too was to lose his life taking part in the sport he loved in Christchurch, New Zealand, on 26 January 1935.

New Cross went on to meet and defeat Walthamstow in the semi-final to find themselves up against West Ham in the final, who themselves had pulled off a surprise semi-final victory against the mighty Wembley.

The first leg, held at the Old Kent Road, was won by the home team 62–44. Farndon won his first five races but, unfortunately, fell in his last. The second leg, at Custom House, was a thriller and was won by West Ham by just a single point, leaving New Cross London Cup champions at their first attempt by a score of 114 to 97.

1 August 1934, New Cross: British Individual Match Race Championship

1: Tom Farndon, Vic Huxley, 59.4 secs (track record)
2: Farndon, Huxley, 60.2 secs

45

1 August 1934: New Cross *v.* Harringay, London Cup First Round Second Leg

NEW CROSS		1	2	3	4	5	6	Total
1	Ron Johnson (Capt.)	3	3	3	2	3	0	14
2	Nobby Key	2	1	2	0	R	1	6
3	Tom Farndon	2	3	3	3	2	3	16
4	Stan Greatrex	3	2	1	2	0	1	9
5	Joe Francis	1	3	0	1	2	3	10
6	George Newton	3	2	1	2	1	2	11
7	Roy Dook (Res.)	–	–	–	–	–	–	–
8	Harry Shepherd (Res.)	–	–	–	–	–	–	–

HARRINGAY		1	2	3	4	5	6	Total
1	Jack Parker (Capt.)	1	1	3	1	1	0	7
2	Norman Parker	0	0	2	3	3	1	9
3	Phil Bishop	0	0	0	0	3	–	3
4	Norman Evans	1	1	1	1	3	2	9
5	Frank Arthur	0	0	0	–	–	–	0
6	Charlie Blacklock	2	2	2	3	R	2	11
7	Cliff Parkinson (Res.)	0	2	0	–	–	–	2
8	Billy Dallison (Res.)	0	–	–	–	–	–	0

Heat 1: Johnson, Key, J. Parker, N. Parker, 65.0 secs
Heat 2: Greatrex, Farndon, Evans, Bishop, 67.4 secs
Heat 3: Newton, Blacklock, Francis, Arthur, 67.0 secs
Heat 4: Farndon, Greatrex, J. Parker, N. Parker, 66.8 secs
Heat 5: Francis, Newton, Evans, Bishop, 68.0 secs
Heat 6: Johnson, Blacklock, Key, Arthur, 66.4 secs
Heat 7: J. Parker, N. Parker, Newton, Francis, 64.8 secs
Heat 8: Johnson, Key, Evans, Parkinson, 66.6 secs
Heat 9: Farndon, Blacklock, Greatrex, Arthur, 64.4 secs
Heat 10: N. Parker, Johnson, J. Parker, Key, 66.0 secs
Heat 11: Farndon, Greatrex, Evans, Bishop, 66.4 secs
Heat 12: Blacklock, Newton, Francis, Dallison, 65.8 secs
Heat 13: N. Parker, Farndon, J. Parker, Greatrex, 64.6 secs
Heat 14: Evans, Francis, Newton, Bishop, 67.0 secs
Heat 15: Johnson, Parkinson, Key (ret.), Blacklock (ret.), 68.2 secs
Heat 16: Francis, Newton, N. Parker, J. Parker, 71.2 secs
Heat 17: Bishop, Evans, Key, Johnson, 66.6 secs
Heat 18: Farndon, Blacklock, Greatrex, Parkinson, 64.6 secs

11 July 1946

Wembley *v.* West Ham: London Cup First Round Second Leg

In the opening paragraph of his report for the *Speedway Gazette* on the Wembley *v.* West Ham London Cup first round second leg of 11 July 1946, the well-respected speedway journalist Tom Morgan said: 'As in other sports so in speedway racing – there will always be classic meetings. Wembley's Empire Stadium has staged many memorable sporting events… but the clash between the Lions and West Ham last Thursday gets the gold medal as the classic of classics. Rarely, if ever, has there been such a thrill-packed, sensational, all-on-the-last-heat eighteen races as in this London Cup tie.'

With the resumption of team speedway in 1946 following the Second World War, the Speedway Control Board pooled all the riders who had declared themselves available for the season and then allocated them on an equitable basis from a pool so that no team would be too strong. All teams were allowed to pick two riders from their pre-war line-up before the allocations began, with the teams taking it in turns to draw one rider at a time from the pool. All the riders were graded into five different categories, with those in grade one being the best. Each team was allowed only one grade one rider.

Alec Jackson, who had ridden at the first meeting at Belle Vue and was now the Wembley manager, had decided to rely on his own resources rather than the pool and had been busy since his demob from the army in 1945 running a training school at Rye House. After choosing his pre-war riders, Tommy Price and George Wilks, and his grade one rider, Bill Kitchen, Jackson chose just one more rider from the pool, Bob Wells, before deciding to withdraw from the allocations and announce he would use four of his own junior discoveries to fill the rest of the places, these being Roy Craighead, Bill Gilbert, Alf Bottoms and Bronco Wilson. Another Rye House discovery, Split Waterman, was later to join the Lions. It was a brave move but it was to pay dividends for Wembley as they dominated the first ten years of post-war speedway in this country and the first trophy of the new era up for grabs was the London Cup.

The London Cup had begun in 1930 and had become, by the time speedway was suspended in 1939, one of the leading competitions in the speedway calendar, ranked only behind the National League and the National Trophy. With the restart of speedway in 1946, the London Cup once again became a much sought-after trophy. The reason for its significance, of course, was that at that time, London was the centre of British speedway and, apart from Belle Vue, all the leading clubs in the National League were in the capital so its importance was only marginally less than that of the National Trophy.

The first leg of this particular first round London Cup tie had been held two days earlier at Custom House, home of the West Ham Hammers, and had resulted in a

Programme cover.

The 1946 Wembley Lions team. From left to right: Tommy Price, Charlie May, T. Barnett (trainer), Roy Craighead, Bill Gilbert, Bill Kitchen (captain), Alec Jackson (manager), Alf Bottoms, Bronco Wilson, Bob Wells, George Wilks.

62-46 win for West Ham. Wembley therefore had a sixteen-point deficit to pull back on their home track. Eric Chitty and former Lion, Colin Watson, had been in great form for the Hammers, scoring 17 and 10 respectively. The *Speedway and Ice News* reported that the 'hero of the night was undoubtedly veteran Colin Watson who delighted the crowd with his brilliant broadsiding and outstanding victories over his opponents', while the *Speedway Gazette* had this to say about Eric Chitty: 'Chitty confounded the powerful Lions with some brilliant individual riding', as well as 'giving a fine display of team riding shepherding home the second strings for much needed vital points. Kitchen, Wilks and Price tried desperately hard to hold their rivals but the Wembley second-strings were completely eclipsed by West Ham's clever team riding. Chitty's promptings were definitely masterly.'

Watson was enjoying something of an indian summer to his career. One of the High Beech pioneers, he had captained Wembley before the Second World War but had been allocated to West Ham on speedway's resumption in 1946 and was now, at the age of forty-seven, being looked on as one of the veterans of the sport. He was, in fact, one of the few top-class riders persisting with the old leg-trailing style of riding and in so doing was keeping the East End crowds on their toes with some breathtaking racing, leading to some magnificent double-point hauls. Not as spectacular, Chitty nevertheless was proving to be an outstanding team captain and it was expected that these two would carry this form on to the Empire Stadium and make it very difficult for the Lions to pull back such a large deficit. In addition, during that meeting, the Wembley reserve, Bronco Wilson, had been stretchered off the track and, although he was able to make a comeback later in the meeting, he was deemed unfit for the second leg and his place was taken by novice George Bason.

The attendance at West Ham was 62,000. Unbelievably this figure was easily eclipsed two days later when 85,000 people turned up for the second leg. The noise

Left: Roy Craighead. His herculean effort to push home for half a lap in heat six was a turning point in the match.

Opposite: Bill Kitchen, the Wembley captain, whose last-heat 5-1 with Tommy Price secured the match for the Lions.

and atmosphere throughout the meeting was just incredible and resembled more a World final, or even an FA Cup final, rather than just a first round match in the London Cup or, as Tom Morgan put it: 'A record, perspiring crowd screamed themselves hoarse.'

Much to the delight of the home crowd, the opening heat was won by Tommy Price with George Wilks following close behind to give a 5-1 to the home team. Heat two saw a 4-2 to Wembley but this was cancelled out in the following heat when Tommy Price fell, giving Malcolm Craven and Benny King, who had replaced Cyril Anderson, a 4-2 for the Hammers. The next heat, heat four, saw Benny King out again, this time in a scheduled ride. On the last lap, Bason fell and the referee stopped the race, ordering a rerun with the exclusion of the rider in red (Bason); there was no thought of awarding races in those days. For King this meant having to complete twelve laps in two races! With Wembley only putting up one rider, the Hammers were able to gain a 4-2 thanks to a victory by Ron Howes over Charlie May, but even worse for the Lions was the fact that Bason was taken to hospital suffering from concussion, leaving Wembley with just six riders for the rest of the night. It looked as though Wembley were now really going to have their work cut out to pull back that sixteen-point deficit.

Tommy Price.

And so it initially proved, as heat five saw another 4-2 to the Hammers with Craven and Chitty doing the honours, so that at the end of this heat the scores on the night were back to all square.

In a curious heat six, during which all four riders experienced machine problems of one sort or another, the Wembley fightback began in earnest. The race was won by Price, who finished with a flat tyre. In second place was Watson, who coasted home after his machine cut out on the last bend. Third was Roy Craighead, whose bike packed up on the back straight of the last lap but made a herculean effort to push home for a half a lap for a vital point, 'shedding bits of machinery all over the track as he went', according to the *Speedway Gazette*, though Roy remembers the incident slightly differently: 'The report was a bit of an exaggeration. I wasn't shedding bits all over the track. What I did was to whip the chain off to free the clutch as they didn't free up on their own like they do these days.' The West Ham reserve, Buck Whitby, had already retired with engine failure earlier in the race. Because of Craighead's determination, Wembley were now back in a two-point lead on the night, but still had fourteen points to make up in twelve heats. Two more Wembley 4-2s followed, with Wilks beating Bob Harrison in heat seven and Price getting the best of the hitherto unbeaten Craven in heat eight.

The next three heats were to prove the turning point for the Lions as they rattled off three 5-1s in succession. Chitty was out for West Ham in two of those heats, finishing third in heat nine while in heat eleven he stalled at the gate. His form of just two days earlier seemed to have deserted him completely and he was having a very poor night. It meant that Wembley had now taken the overall lead for the first time. In the middle of this, the jitters were definitely getting to both sides as heat ten had to be started no fewer than four times before the referee was satisfied that the start was fair.

The West Ham star of the evening, Malcolm Craven, like Colin Watson another former Wembley man, was able to stop the rot in heat twelve, beating Tommy Price for a 3-3. With six heats to go, Wembley were now eighteen points in front on the night and two points in front on aggregate.

With the match poised on a knife-edge, heat thirteen proved to be another exciting race as Craighead tried his best to hold off Chitty and Howes but, in his determination to earn his team maximum points, he overdid it on the last lap and fell, causing the race to be stopped and rerun without him, leading to a fairly easy 5-1 for the Hammers, putting them back into the overall lead by two points. With Bason still missing, Wembley's lone competitor in the next heat, Charlie May, put in a supreme effort to defeat Howes and Benny King to share the points. The Hammers' two-point lead remained with just four heats to go. The next heat, however, saw two of Wembley's heat leaders, Bill Kitchen and George Wilks, out against Colin Watson. Watson hardly seemed to be the same rider who had done so well just two days previously and a 5-1 to Wembley saw them now take a two-point lead.

With three heats to go it was nail-biting stuff but, with Howes and Craven, their two best riders on the evening, out in the next three heats – Howes in the next and Craven in the last two – West Ham had high hopes of pulling back the small deficit

West Ham captain Eric Chitty, who had a poor night by his standards.

and running out victors. But the next two heats finished at 3-3, so with one heat to go, Wembley still held their two-point lead and needed a 3-3 to take the tie, while West Ham were far from beaten and could still win with a 5-1. The line-up for that vital heat eighteen saw Price and Kitchen out for Wembley; Craven and Chitty for the Hammers. Craven had already beaten both Kitchen and Price during the meeting and was riding superbly. Unfortunately for West Ham, Chitty was not having a good night, but if he could just recapture his form of two days previously there was still a chance to snatch the necessary last-heat victory, but it did not look promising.

With a crowd of 85,000 roaring on their favourite team, the noise was deafening as the tapes shot up. Amazingly both Price and Kitchen reared, allowing Craven and Chitty the chance to race off in to a clear lead. The Hammers fans in the crowd could not believe it. The impossible suddenly seemed possible. Price was the first to get his bike back under control and he went roaring off, racing into the bends at full throttle. Quickly pegging back Chitty he flew round the outside of him and set off after Craven. He soon caught him up and snapped away at his rear wheel, waiting for his chance. Finally, on the first bend of the last lap, Price's continual harrying and worrying had its desired effect as he forced Craven into making a small mistake as he moved almost imperceptibly away from the white line. But it was enough for Price. In a flash he was through and what was more, Kitchen, who had passed Chitty earlier in the race, was just behind and followed Price through the gap, turning a West Ham 5-1 into a Wembley 5-1. As the chequered flag fell at the end of the race, the whole stadium erupted. Heat eighteen had probably been the best race anyone in the crowd had ever seen. The fans shouted themselves hoarse, demanding laps of honour from Price and Kitchen and the whole Wembley team. It was many minutes before the announcer could make the official announcement giving the result.

Perhaps the strangest evening's racing belonged to Ron Howes as twice he won a rerun race having already completed four laps, and he was also one of the participants in the four-times-started heat ten. Nevertheless, he was the only Hammer apart from Craven to make any impression on the Lions, finishing with a total of nine points.

Sadly this was to be Colin Watson's last full match as, two days later, on 13 July, he was badly injured in a crash at Bradford. In a second-half scratch race he crashed and hit a lighting standard by the safety fence. He half-fell from his machine, which dragged him head down for about twenty yards. He was rushed to hospital with a fractured skull and a punctured lung. He lay unconscious for many days. Although he eventually recovered he was never to ride again and the career of one of the greatest British riders of all time was over.

It may have been fate or some sort of speedway equivalent to 'the laying on of hands' that West Ham's new star and successor to Watson, who had so nearly kept the

Malcolm Craven was the only West Ham rider to show his true form that night, scoring a total of 15 points.

Hammers' London Cup hopes alive that night, was Malcolm Craven, as he would often speak with unashamed hero worship of the days when, as a schoolboy before the Second World War, he had had the privilege of carrying Colin Watson's leathers at Wembley and had been the beneficiary of much sound advice from the great man.

Wembley went on to take the London Cup and begin their domination of British speedway by beating Wimbledon in the final by the convincing score of 121 to 95, having won both legs, though the two matches were not without incident. In the first at Plough Lane one heat had to be rerun after all four riders broke through the tapes on seeing a photographer's flash as they thought the bright light was the gate rising.

The second leg at Wembley, witnessed by yet another large crowd of almost 80,000, saw two spectacular crashes. In the first, Kitchen and Lloyd Goffe were stretchered off after colliding and being flung across the track. In the second, Wimbledon's Dick Harris came tearing out of the first bend in heat thirteen, was forced wide and crashed into the safety fence. He found himself wedged between the track and the board of the fence, and while struggling attendants and ambulance men fought to extricate him, the other riders came round on their second lap. In exactly the same spot, Craighead swerved towards the fence. In a desperate, almost super-human effort, he wrestled his machine back under control and just managed to avoid crashing into the fallen Harris and his rescuers, averting what would have been a very nasty incident.

But to return to that first-leg match, as we started with the first paragraph of Tom Morgan's report in the *Speedway Gazette*, it seems appropriate to finish this chapter with his last paragraph: 'If only for the sensational last heat, Wembley well deserved their win. When they found themselves pressed during the last couple of heats they pulled out that little something extra that gives speedway racing its curious appeal to the ever-growing multitude. One could say that this match, with its tense electric atmosphere and a crowd comparable with any major sporting event in the world, was one of the finest advertisements the sport has ever had.'

11 July 1946: Wembley *v.* West Ham: London Speedway Cup First Round Second Leg:

WEMBLEY		1	2	3	4	5	6	Total
1	Bill Kitchen (Capt.)	3	2	3	2	3	2	15
2	Roy Craighead	1	1	3	X	1	–	6
3	Tommy Price	3	0	3	3	2	3	14
4	Alf Bottoms	0	1	2	1	3	–	7
5	George Wilks	2	3	3	2	2	–	12
6	Bob Wells	2	1	2	1	0	–	6
7	George Bason (Res.)	X	–	–	–	–	–	0
8	Charlie May (Res.)	2	3	–	–	–	–	5

WEST HAM		1	2	3	4	5	6	Total
1	Eric Chitty (Capt.)	0	1	1	0	2	0	4
2	Malcolm Craven	3	3	2	3	3	1	15
3	Buck Whitby	1	R	0	–	–	–	1
4	Colin Watson	0	2	1	0	1	–	4
5	Cyril Anderson	0	0	–	–	–	–	0
6	Bob Harrison	2	2	0	2	0	–	6
7	Benny King (Res.)	1	1	1	1	–	–	4
8	Ron Howes (Res.)	3	0	1	3	2	–	9

Heat 1: Price, Wilks, Whitby, Chitty, 78.2 secs
Heat 2: Kitchen, Harrison, Craighead, Watson, 78.0 secs
Heat 3: Craven, Wells, King, Price, 78.6 secs
Heat 4 (Rerun): Howes, May, King, Bason (f/exc), 81.0 secs
Heat 5: Craven, Kitchen, Chitty, Bottoms, 76.4 secs
Heat 6: Price, Watson, Craighead (e/f pushed home), Whitby (e/f), 81.3 secs
Heat 7: Wilks, Harrison, Bottoms, Anderson, 79.8 secs
Heat 8: Kitchen, Craven, Wells, Howes, 77.4 secs
Heat 9: Price, Kitchen, Chitty, Harrison, 78.4 secs
Heat 10: Craighead, Bottoms, Howes, Whitby, 81.4 secs
Heat 11: Wilks, Wells, Watson, Chitty, 81.2 secs
Heat 12: Craven, Price, Bottoms, Watson, 78.0 secs
Heat 13 (Rerun): Howes, Chitty, Wells, Craighead (f/exc), 81.0 secs
Heat 14: May, Howes, King, Bason (ns), 81.6 secs
Heat 15: Kitchen, Wilks, Watson, Anderson, 80.4 secs
Heat 16: Bottoms, Harrison, King, Wells, 82.2 secs
Heat 17: Craven, Wilks, Craighead, Harrison, 79.6 secs
Heat 18: Price, Kitchen, Craven, Chitty, 79.2 secs

9 June 1947: Newcastle

The Speedway Riders' Championship Second Round

The speedway World Championship was inaugurated in 1936 and held during the remaining pre-war years. When speedway resumed in this country after the Second World War many of the top Australians and Americans did not return immediately so, instead of continuing the World Championship, a new event was held in 1946, called the British Riders' Championship. In 1947 the name was changed to the Speedway Riders' Championship to reflect the fact that more and more overseas riders were returning to these shores (although, the programme for the Newcastle round of the championship still calls it the British Riders' Championship). As with the World Championship a number of qualifying rounds were held to find the sixteen who would fight it out at Wembley on final night. In 1947 there were three divisions, so the championship started with rounds at the Third Division tracks. From there a number of qualifiers joined Second Division riders for the second round held on Second Division tracks.

Second Division Newcastle held its meeting on 9 June. Among those down to take part was the Wigan rider, Norman Hargreaves. However, Hargreaves failed to appear at Newcastle's Brough Park track and so, just before the meeting was due to start, Newcastle reserve Alec 'Farmer' Grant was pressed into service. The Newcastle promotion and fans were not looking for big things from Grant. In that night's programme it seemed he did not give much thought to actually winning races. In his page in the programme ('Johnnie's Jottings'), promoter Johnnie Hoskins discussed the team spirit that was becoming clear in the Newcastle team. He reported that when asked for the quickest way round Brough Park, the top riders were only too keen to give some good advice to the youngsters. However, this is how Hoskins described Alec's advice: 'Farmer Grant though does it differently. He just shakes his head and laughs. "Don't ask me for advice. I don't know myself how I get round. Charlie Spinks told me to keep trying, keep on falling and one day you'll win lots of races. That's all I know."' Not a very inspiring statement and not one to give great confidence that he actually was going to go out and win his races! In fact, to look at Grant you would not think he was a speedway rider at all. He was one of the biggest and heaviest men ever to sit on a speedway bike and, as if that wasn't handicap enough, the young farmer only had one good eye.

Among the favourites to win the meeting were the three Newcastle heat leaders, Doug McLachlan, Norman Evans and Wilf Jay, and former Newcastle rider and now Glasgow captain, Will Lowther. Lowther still lived locally and had in fact ridden at Brough Park the week before as Newcastle had taken on Glasgow in a National Trophy fixture. He had scored an eighteen-point maximum with some ease apart from the very last heat of the match when he was up against Grant and McLachlan. The two

Right: Programme cover.

Below: Alec 'Farmer' Grant.

Newcastle riders had gated first and although Lowther had flown past Grant with relatively little difficulty, it had taken him almost all four laps to catch the Newcastle number one, finally managing to get past in the last few yards. The Brough Park faithful were hoping that Lowther would not be so successful in the Riders' Championship round and that one of their own would put him in his place. Little did they suspect which of their own it would be who would come closest to doing just that.

With the late withdrawal of Hargreaves, Grant hardly had time to get his leathers on before he was called to the tapes to take his place in heat one. Up against three of the Second Division's leading riders, Ted Bravery, Stan Dell and his own team's number one, Doug McLachlan, he wasn't expected to do much more than make up the numbers. But this was not how Farmer Grant saw it and, much to the surprise of the 12,000-strong crowd, he roared away from the start to win the race in what turned out to be the fastest time of the night.

Out again in heat eight he found himself up against Laurie Packer, Sid Hipperson and Harwood Pike, all of whom had failed to score in their first race. Maybe this time it wasn't too much of a surprise that Grant, on his own track, should get the better of these three. Nevertheless it meant that after two rides each, only two riders remained unbeaten, Grant and Gateshead-born Glasgow Tigers star and captain, Will Lowther.

Heat twelve saw Grant taking on much stronger opposition in his own Newcastle captain, Norman Evans, Birmingham's Bob Lovell, who had won his first race and old stager Percy Brine of Wigan. Shortly after the start Brine and Grant tangled and both were thrown to the ground. The race was stopped and rerun with Brine adjudged to be the cause of the accident and excluded. Grant was completely unperturbed by this little mix-up and in the rerun found himself involved in one of the most exciting races of the night as Evans got away at the start from Grant with Lovell closely behind. Grant worried away at his captain for two laps, trying first inside and then outside, while Lovell was doing much the same to him. As they came round the first bend on the third lap, Grant just rode flat out round the outside of Evans and with an amazing turn of speed shot out of the second bend and up the back straight with a clear lead. There was no catching him now and, to the delight of the Newcastle crowd, he went on to win the race. Three rides, nine points.

In his fourth ride the still-unbeaten farmer from Westerhope was up against Wilf Jay, whose only defeat in three rides at come at the hands of Lowther, the night's only other unbeaten rider, the Wigan skipper Jack Gordon, who had won his second ride and fellow Newcastle reserve Ken Le Breton, who had also won his previous race. Grant was not overawed and, as the tapes went up, he gained the advantage and held on round the first bend. Jay stuck close to him round the first lap with the other two losing ground. Jay was a master of the Newcastle track and knew his way round as well as, if not better than, any other rider. He was one of the leading riders in the Second Division and almost unbeatable at Brough Park. He was later to finish the season as fourth-highest scorer in the league. But, that night, try as he might, he was unable to find a way past his own junior. Grant stuck to his line and made no mistakes, holding off Jay to take the chequered flag, leaving him going into his last ride still unbeaten.

The 1947 Newcastle team. From left to right: Wilf Jay, Alec Grant, Jack Hunt, Norman Evans (on bike), Johnnie Hoskins (Promoter), Doug McLachlan, Ken Le Breton, Peter Lloyd, Bonnie Waddell.

So far it had been an incredible night for the farmer. Four rides, four wins. Will Lowther had also continued his winning ways and now the scene was set for the showdown finale as the two met in the last heat of the night. The other two riders in the race were no push-overs either: Middlesbrough's Jack Hodgson had seven points and Norwich's Paddy Mills had eight.

As the tapes rose for this final heat, it was Lowther who was first away, beating Grant into the first bend, but the farmer held his throttle wide open riding full pelt round the outside. He narrowed the gap down the back straight and then, incredibly, passed Lowther on the fourth bend, entering the home straight in the lead. The crowd were going wild as their new hero seemed all set to take the heat and a maximum fifteen points. The noise round the track was staggering as the crowd roared him on. Coming into the first bend on the second lap, Grant cut across to the inside with a clear lead, which he held down the back straight. But then, disaster! To the great frustration of the crowd, Grant overslid on the third bend and fell. A great groan went up from all round the track as Lowther slipped past and romped home to win in easy style.

The round and the £50 winner's cheque belonged to Lowther, but the evening most certainly belonged to the local junior Alec Grant. As Lowther came forward to receive his cheque the crowd chanted: 'We want Alec! We want Alec!' So persistent did this become that promoter Johnnie Hoskins had to call over the Westerhope farmer to the microphone before the fans would quieten down.

This was not the end of Grant's fairytale evening, however, as in the second half he qualified for the final of the handicap event. Because of his score in the main event and because he won his heat of the handicap he was put at the back in the final and it seemed

Glasgow's Will Lowther, the winner of the 1947
Newcastle Riders' Championship round.

that he was hopelessly handicapped out of the reckoning. But this was Alec Grant's night
and he went on to win the final in great style to complete a memorable night.

Although not present at the meeting in 1947, former promoter Dick Barrie
remembers Alec Grant well: 'I saw Alec 'Farmer' Grant briefly in 1949, after which I
think he dropped off the scene, as more younger riders took up the sport and with
tracks beginning to close down after the first boom period, team places became
tougher to hold onto. What had happened was that the Middlesbrough team, which
had been too successful for their own good, were moved en bloc to Newcastle at the
end of 1948. The existing Newcastle club, now homeless, moved north to open
Ashfield in Glasgow. Although only a boy when I was aware of Alec at Ashfield I have
seen some 16mm film from these days, in which he displayed all the rough-and-tumble
aggression I recall! I met him years later, around 1977, when I was working for
Berwick speedway and he brought his son Robert to the track to try out for the
Bandits. Rob progressed into the Berwick team, for whom he raced with distinction
until the early 1990s, captaining the club to several KO Cup successes. His own son
(also Rob) has now taken up the mantle and rides for Stoke Potters. The Grants are
thus one of only two direct-line three-generation families of speedway riders to
perform in the UK at league level (the other being the Allott family, represented by
grandfather Guy, son Nicky and grandson Adam). Alec raised pigs, I recall – hence
'Farmer' – and after he had retired, and later seen Rob's career launched, he took a

Newcastle's number one in 1947, Doug McLachlan.

back seat and rarely came to the tracks. He died some years ago. My childish eyes regarded him as a fearsome on-track warrior, and my adult memories recall him as a pleasant, somewhat gruff old man!'

Ian Hoskins, son of Newcastle promoter Johnnie Hoskins, who was himself promoter of Lowther's Glasgow team, recalls of Alec Grant that 'he was a farmer who had only one eye. My riders always knew that it was unwise to try and pass him on his blind side as you were liable to be fenced. He was a bit of a wild man anyway and a true track personality of his day, even if his potential was limited by his handicap.'

Ian Hoskins also had this to say about his own captain: 'Will Lowther was the original captain of Glasgow Tigers in 1946. He and Joe Crowther were known to the crowd as the 'terrible twins', simply because of their names. Lowther, however, was a rider who had a 'gammy' left leg. No-one was allowed to see it in the dressing room. He used to change early ahead of the rest. When riding, his left leg was always stiff and straight, but he was a reliable heat leader during his day. When the youngsters such as Bainbridge, Tommy Miller and the others caught up with him, he retired to Newcastle to become a promoter. In fact, I purchased Frank Hodgson from him for a then-record £1,000 fee for the Tigers. Crowther was by far the more enigmatic rider and would have a go from anywhere. Lowther tended to be a stylist who rode to his own limitations.'

By one of those quirks of the fixture list, Lowther was back at Brough Park yet again the following week, this time in a National League Second Division fixture. Once more he scored a maximum. In all, he rode in fifteen races at Newcastle in three consecutive meetings and won every one of them.

Will Lowther went on to qualify for the First Division round of the Riders' Championship, scoring seven at Norwich, thirteen on his own Glasgow track and twelve at Sheffield to finish in third place behind Frank Hodgson and Fred Curtis. Poor Alec had no other rounds to compete in. His role was confined to meeting reserve at Newcastle. And if Norman Hargreaves had turned up that fateful evening, Grant would never have had the chance to show what he could do.

Never again did Alec Grant perform like that. It was a one-off. He finished the season with a match average for Newcastle of 5.45. The following season it rose to 6.10 but that was about as good as it got for the young farmer from Westerhope apart from that one astonishing night at Newcastle in June 1947 when he took on and beat some of the best riders in the Second Division including all three of his own team's heat-leaders.

There was one other significant event that evening that almost went unnoticed in the events surrounding Alec Grant's sensational evening. A young Australian by the name of Ken Le Breton, who had only been transferred to Newcastle from New Cross less than a month earlier on 16 May 1947, was also pressed into service as a meeting reserve for another non-arrival, Tiger Hart. In his third race, Le Breton beat Ted Bravery, Jack Hodgson and Harwood Pike, to record his first-ever win at Brough Park. Le Breton went on to become an Australian Test star, qualifying for the first post-war World Championship final in 1949. Sadly, he was another who was to die tragically on the track on 5 January 1951 during an Australia *v.* England Test match at the Sydney Sports Ground.

9 June 1947: Newcastle: British Speedway Riders' Championship Second Round

		1	2	3	4	5	Total
1	Will Lowther	3	3	3	3	3	15
2	Wilf Jay	2	3	3	2	3	13
3	Alec Grant	3	3	3	3	F	12
4	Norman Evans	3	2	2	1	2	10
5	Bob Lovell	3	F	2	1	3	9
6	Jack Hodgson	2	2	0	3	2	9
7	Paddy Mills	2	2	2	2	1	9
8	Doug McLachlan	F	1	1	3	3	8
9	Jack Gordon	1	3	0	1	2	7
10	Ted Bravery	2	1	2	0	1	6
11	Ken Le Breton	1	1	3	0	0	5
12	Sid Hipperson	0	2	0	1	2	5
13	Stan Dell	1	0	1	2	1	5
14	Percy Brine	1	F	F	–	–	3
15	Laurie Packer	0	0	2	0	0	2
16	Harwood Pike	F	1	1	0	0	2
17	Jack Hunt (reserve)	–	1	1	–	–	2

Ken Le Breton, who scored his first race win at Newcastle that night.

Heat 1: Grant, Bravery, Dell, McLachlan (f), 76.2 secs

Heat 2: Lovell, Mills, Le Breton, Packer, 79.2 secs

Heat 3: Evans, Hodgson, Gordon, Hipperson, 77.8 secs

Heat 4: Lowther, Jay, Brine, Pike (f), 77.8 secs

Heat 5: Gordon, Mills, Bravery, Brine (f), 79.6 secs

Heat 6: Lowther, Evans, Le Breton, Dell, 77.2 secs

Heat 7: Jay, Hodgson, McLachlan, Lovell (f), 78.4 secs

Heat 8: Grant, Hipperson, Pike, Packer, 79.8 secs

Heat 9: Le Breton, Bravery, Pike, Hodgson, 80.2 secs

Heat 10: Jay, Mills, Dell, Hipperson, 79.4 secs

Heat 11: Lowther, Lovell, Hipperson, Bravery, 78.4 secs

Heat 12: Grant, Evans, Lovell, Brine (f), 78.2 secs

Heat 13: Lowther, Packer, McLachlan, Gordon, 79.2 secs

Heat 14: Hodgson, Dell, Hunt, Packer, 80.0 secs

Heat 15: McLachlan, Mills, Evans, Pike, 78.4 secs

Heat 16: Grant, Jay, Gordon, Le Breton, 79.4 secs

Heat 17: Jay, Evans, Bravery, Packer, 78.6 secs

Heat 18: Lovell, Gordon, Dell, Pike, 79.0 secs

Heat 19: McLachlan, Hipperson, Hunt, Le Breton, 80.4 secs

Heat 20: Lowther, Hodgson, Mills, Grant (f), 79.0 secs

20 September 1951

Wembley: 1951 World Championship Final

The 1951 World Championship final will forever be associated with two Australian riders: Jack Young, who became the first and only rider from a lower division ever to win the world title and Jack Biggs, for the manner in which he somehow managed to snatch defeat from the jaws of victory.

The World Championship had begun in 1936. In the pre-war years, riders qualified through a series of qualifying rounds and carried bonus points with them into the final based on the number of points they had scored in the qualifying rounds. With the return to Great Britain of the overseas riders, mostly Australians, the World Championship was revived in 1949. Riders still had to go through the qualifying rounds but the bonus points system was dropped, which meant that all riders started the final on equal terms.

In 1951 the first round involved Third Division riders, eighteen of whom qualified for the second round in which they met Second Division riders, one of whom was Jack Young, then riding for Edinburgh. Young topped the qualifiers from round two with an unbeaten thirty points, progressing to the championship round where he and the other Second Division qualifiers were joined by the First Division riders, including Jack Biggs. Young more than held his own with the 'big boys', scoring twelve points at Wimbledon and eleven points at Bristol to finish in seventh place overall. Biggs did even better, scoring a maximum fifteen points on his own track, Harringay, and fourteen at Bradford, to become the top qualifier for the final with twenty-nine points.

Others to qualify for the final included the current champion, Wembley's Fred Williams, along with the three top ranked First Division riders, Split Waterman, Aub Lawson and Ronnie Moore.

It looked all set to become an intriguing final. Could Jack Young, a mere Second Division rider, really mix it with the cream of the speedway world? Could Jack Biggs prove that his position as top qualifier was justified? Would Fred Williams' home track advantage see him become the first rider to win two World Championships? Would the young Wimbledon sensation, the eighteen-year-old Ronnie Moore, show that he had the maturity to continue his outstanding league form in the world's biggest individual event? Or would the skill and experience of the two pre-final favourites, Split Waterman and Aub Lawson, be too much for the others?

In front of 93,000 spectators, the first eagerly awaited clash occurred in the very first heat as Jack Young took on Split Waterman but, in a sensational race, little-fancied Bradford rider and World final debutant Eddie Rigg, who had qualified in last place, held off both of them to take the chequered flag in what turned out to be the fastest time of the night, 70.6 secs. Another upset followed in the second race as

Programme cover.

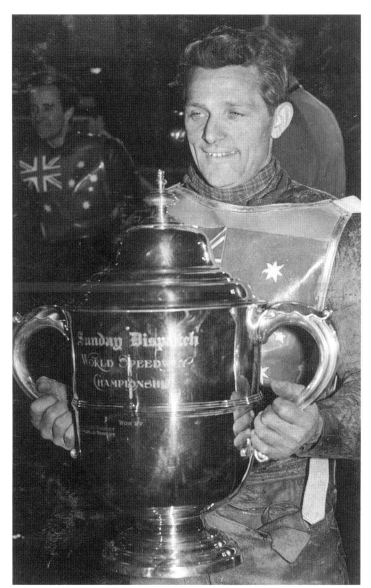

Left: Jack Young holds the *Sunday Dispatch* World Championship Trophy. Jack Biggs can just be seen in the background.

Opposite: Australian Jackie Biggs, who snatched defeat from the jaws of victory.

Aub Lawson was relegated to third place behind Norwich's Bob Leverenz and Wimbledon's American star Ernie Roccio. Normality returned in the third heat as Freddie Williams easily saw off the opposition. Then, in heat four, a sign of things to come, as Jack Biggs shot out the gate ahead of Ronnie Moore and proved to be unstoppable.

Out again in the following heat, Biggs once more flew out of the gate but this time he was closely followed by Jack Young. A terrific battle between the two ensued until Biggs finally made it across the line with barely a length to spare. Heat eight saw Eddie Rigg prove that his first-heat win was no fluke as he once again took the flag, this time

relegating two previous heat winners, Leverenz and Williams, to second and third place respectively. After two rides each therefore, just two riders remained unbeaten, Biggs and Rigg. Leverenz was third on five points, while Young, Moore, Williams and Jeff Lloyd each had four.

The individual race format was different at that period to that in use today and it meant that Young had two more rides before Biggs had even one. With Young winning both of them he forced himself back into the reckoning. Williams came last in his next outing and, with Leverenz and Lloyd trailing in third and fourth respectively in heat thirteen, all three were now, to all intents and purposes, out of the running. Rigg also had a poor third ride, coming third. Biggs, meanwhile, continued on his way. Once again he got flyers at the start of both heats twelve and fourteen, winning both races with some ease. There was no doubt that, on the night, Biggs was the fastest gater there as he won his first four races from the start.

After his third place in the first heat, Waterman's fortunes improved and he won his second and third races, but he dropped another point in his fourth race, coming second to the wily old timer Jack Parker.

At the end of four rides each, Biggs was the only unbeaten rider with twelve points. Behind him were Young on ten, Waterman on nine and Moore on eight. Heat seventeen saw Young and Moore's final ride and, when Young could only manage second place, giving him a total of twelve points for the night, it meant that Biggs needed just one point from his final ride to be sure of victory and the title of world champion 1951.

So far Biggs's gating had been immaculate and heat nineteen seemed a mere formality for him. All he needed was third place, one point, to be sure. Not that the other three riders were push-overs. In fact he was up against three of the pre-meeting favourites in Waterman, Williams and Lawson, but both Williams and Lawson had not had good nights, going into this important race with just six and five points respectively.

As the tapes headed skyward, however, it was Lawson who jetted out of the gate. For the first time that night and in such a crucial race, Biggs failed to get away first. Instead he trapped in second place. Being drawn in gate four he attempted to drive round Lawson on the first bend, but he drifted disastrously wide allowing both Williams and Waterman to slip by on the inside. Blinded by the shale being thrown in his face by the other bikes as they roared away from him, Biggs found himself in a hopeless position and was unable to make up any ground. As they entered the second lap, Lawson was still in front with Williams in second place and Waterman third. Waterman's lightning brain quickly calculated that, with Biggs trailing in last place, he would still have a chance of the title if he could win the race. Quickly taking Williams, he set off in pursuit of Lawson. Lawson held the lead until the final bend when a determined do-or-die effort from Waterman saw him ride right round the boards, gaining enough speed to pass Lawson on the run-in, just snatching victory on the line. It was undoubtedly the best race of the night but a disaster for Biggs.

Second-placed Split Waterman was involved in both the races that sealed Biggs's fate.

In spite of his disappointing last place, all was not lost for Biggs as he now shared the lead with Young and Waterman, all on twelve points, and a run-off was needed to determine who would be World Champion. The draw for the run-off saw Waterman on the inside, Biggs in the middle and Young on the outside. As they came up to the tapes the tension in the stadium was almost unbearable. Apart from the diehard supporters of Waterman and Young, many in the crowd felt some sympathy for Biggs and he received extra cheers as he motored out of the pits and up to the start line.

As the tapes rose, Biggs seemed to have regained his earlier form and he flew away from the start in first place. Young trapped behind him but Waterman had a very poor start. Young worried away at Biggs all the way round the first lap and got his reward on the second as Biggs drifted wide and he was able to get by on the inside. Once in front, Young steadily pulled away from his hapless fellow countryman to take the chequered flag and the title of 1951 world champion. But there was even worse to come for Biggs as Waterman continued to make up ground after his dreadful start and, on the last bend, charged past the disconsolate Aussie to take away even the runner-up spot. Needing just one point in his last race to be champion, Biggs now found himself finishing in overall third place.

There has been much speculation in the speedway world about that fateful heat nineteen. Was Biggs overcome by nerves or was there an even more sinister explanation for his poor showing? It has been said, for example, that Aub Lawson went to the other two riders before the race and asked them if Jackie had 'said anything' to them. They replied that he had not. The inference was that Lawson at least had expected Biggs to say something to them along the lines that he needed only one point and to ask them to 'cover' for him, which, in speedway riders' code, means 'stay out of the way!' The story goes that when Biggs said nothing to the others they decided to 'fix' him, because they felt he had been too arrogant to ask for any help, which is precisely what they did by taking him out on the first bend. Biggs himself confided some years later that he asked for nothing because he was so confident he could win the race that he did not need to ask for any favours from anyone. In the circumstances this does not seem unreasonable on Biggs' part. He had been by far the fastest gater of the evening. Lawson and Williams were having poor evenings. Lawson in particular seemed to lack his usual verve, probably because of a hand injury he had sustained at Liverpool four days before the final. Biggs should have won, or at the very worst come second to Waterman, on his own merits. It was unthinkable to imagine him not getting at least third place and that somehow, just because he had not asked for any favours, Lawson and Williams would be able to beat him.

Nerves seem a much more plausible explanation for his poor gating in that heat. And it was this plus his outside draw that did for him. Biggs' draw for the evening was number thirteen. For the superstitious, that may be explanation enough for what happened to him, but being number thirteen also meant that he had a long gap between his last two races. Time for those nerves to get the better of him. Plenty of time for all the well-wishers in and around the pits to congratulate him prematurely and set him off thinking that the title of world champion was almost as good as his. Eric Linden, the doyen of speedway journalists, said after the meeting: 'Why couldn't the well-wishers leave well alone?'

Ken Taylor, a speedway fan who was there that night, said that when Biggs came out for his last heat everyone thought it was all over but, of course, it was not. His view of those two final races was that it was nerves that beat him: 'Biggs was a very nervous man. I remember seeing him in the pits some years later in a London Riders' Championship final when again he was in with a chance of winning. He was a bag of nerves; his hands were shaking so much I was surprised he could hold his bike up! There was one other problem facing Biggsie that no-one else ever mentions but I think it was significant and that was that he was up against three riders who were not only world-class but had all ridden for Wembley, so they knew the track like the backs of their hands. With Biggs not making the gate in heat nineteen, they were able to outmanoeuvre him and fill him in. By the time of the run-off, although he did get the gate, his nerves were just shot to pieces. It was a shame but, in some ways, as it turned out, Youngie was probably a more worthy world champion.'

Former world champion Tommy Price, who was at Wembley as BBC TV's inter-race commentator, said: 'I must say I feel sorry for Jack Biggs. After winning those races

Aub Lawson, gated ahead of Biggs in the all-important heat nineteen.

in such brilliant style, getting pushed out of the first bend of his fifth race and then finishing last, must have been a blow to him, and then to lead the deciding heat for the first lap and fall back must have been the last straw.' Price's advice to Biggs, however, was to remain optimistic: 'Have another go next year, faint heart never won fair lady, don't forget.'

But it was not to be. In spite of a long racing career, which included two more World final appearances, he was never again to get so close to glory. Like Farndon, Blacklock and Le Breton before him, Biggs eventually lost his life doing what he loved best on the track at Bendigo in Australia on 9 December 1972. Jack Young, meanwhile, became the toast of Edinburgh and the whole of the Second Division. He had shown that not only could he mix it with the big boys but he could beat them all. It was, of course, a bittersweet moment for Edinburgh as it was obvious that Young would now look for a bigger club and, sure enough, he signed up for First Division West Ham before the 1952 season started. At the following year's World Championship final he proved that his win in 1951 was no fluke by becoming the first rider to win the World Championship twice and forever afterwards being spoken of as one of, if not the, greatest riders of all time.

One final footnote to this extraordinary final: although he did not get a ride, Aldershot's Geoff Mardon, second reserve on the night, became the only Third Division rider ever to appear in the line-up for a World Championship final.

20 September 1951: Wembley: 1951 World Speedway Championship Final

		1	2	3	4	5	Total
1	Jack Young	2	2	3	3	2	12
2	Split Waterman	1	3	3	2	3	12
3	Jack Biggs	3	3	3	3	0	12
4	Ronnie Moore	2	2	2	2	3	11
5	Jack Parker	0	1	3	3	3	10
6	Louis Lawson	2	0	2	3	3	10
7	Eddie Rigg	3	3	1	1	0	8
8	Bob Leverenz	3	2	1	0	1	7
9	Freddie Williams	3	1	0	2	1	7
10	Aub Lawson	1	2	2	0	2	7
11	Jeff Lloyd	1	3	1	0	1	6
12	Eric Williams	0	1	1	2	2	6
13	Cyril Brine	1	R	2	0	0	3
14	Norman Parker	0	1	1	1	0	3
15	Ernie Roccio	2	0	0	R	–	2
16	Alan Hunt	F	F	0	1	1	2
17	Dick Bradley (Res.)	2	–	–	–	–	2
18	Geoff Mardon (Res.)	–	–	–	–	–	0

The 1950 champion Freddie Williams, the other rider involved in heat nineteen.

Heat 1: Rigg, Young, Waterman, N. Parker, 70.6 secs

Heat 2: Leverenz, Roccio, A. Lawson, J. Parker, 71.0

Heat 3: F. Williams, L. Lawson, Brine, E. Williams, 70.8 secs

Heat 4: Biggs, Moore, Lloyd, Hunt (f), 71.6 secs

Heat 5: Biggs, Young, J. Parker, L. Lawson, 70.6 secs

Heat 6: Lloyd, A. Lawson, N. Parker, Brine (ret.), 71.4 secs

Heat 7: Waterman, Moore, E. Williams, Roccio, 71.4 secs

Heat 8: Rigg, Leverenz, F. Williams, Hunt (f), 71.6 secs

Heat 9: Young, A. Lawson, E. Williams, Hunt, 70.6 secs

Heat 10: J. Parker, Moore, N. Parker, F. Williams, 71.4 secs

Heat 11: Young, F. Williams, Lloyd, Roccio, 71.4 secs

Heat 12: Biggs, Brine, Rigg, Roccio (r), 71.8 secs

Heat 13: Waterman, L. Lawson, Leverenz, Lloyd, 72.2 secs

Heat 14: Biggs, E. Williams, N. Parker, Leverenz, 72.2 secs

Heat 15: J. Parker, Waterman, Hunt, Brine, 72.4 secs

Heat 16: L. Lawson, Moore, Rigg, A. Lawson, 71.8 secs

Heat 17: Moore, Young, Leverenz, Brine, 72.0 secs

Heat 18: L. Lawson, Bradley, Hunt, N. Parker, 73.2 secs

Heat 19: Waterman, A. Lawson, F. Williams, Biggs, 73.2 secs

Heat 20: J. Parker, E. Williams, Lloyd, Rigg, 73.8 secs

Heat 21 (Run-off for first place): Young, Waterman, Biggs, 72.6 secs

7 August 1957

Norwich *v.* Belle Vue: Britannia Shield Final Second Leg
and Golden Helmet Match Race Championship Second Leg

Following the death of Tom Farndon, the British Match Race Championship was abandoned and was not restarted until after the Second World War when Bill Kitchen was nominated as the new champion in 1946. At the start of the 1957 season the title was held by Belle Vue's Peter Craven. His first challenger was Barry Briggs, who he defeated by two legs to one. As the name, British Match Race Championship, implied, it was open only to British riders, although this was liberally interpreted to include Australians and New Zealanders. However, the match the public wanted to see was between Craven and the 1956 World Champion, Norwich's Ove Fundin, a Swede. To enable this to take place, the Speedway Control Board changed both the rules and the name of the competition. The competition became the Golden Helmet Match Race Championship and all riders riding in British leagues were allowed to take part.

Before he could get at Craven however, Fundin had to face an eliminator against Southampton's England ace, Brian Crutcher. Having come through this successfully, he faced the champion at the latter's home track, Belle Vue, on 20 July 1957. Unfortunately for Fundin he suffered machine trouble in his first race as his engine cut out on the second lap and he was forced to retire. For the second race he borrowed teammate Phil Clarke's machine but was never in the race, finally going down by sixty yards.

The second leg took place on Fundin's home track, Norwich, on 7 August. Craven won the toss and took the inside position. Fundin gated first but Craven took him on the first bend. From then on he was never in any real trouble and by the end of the race held a fourteen-length lead. Fundin was now one leg down and 1-0 down in the second.

The second race saw Fundin on the inside. He again gated first; this time however, he held his lead round the first and second bends and led going into the back straight. The spectacular Craven chased after him and at one point managed to draw level, but Fundin quickly dropped onto the white line and from then on remained glued to it, finishing the race ten lengths in front.

Fundin won the toss for the decider and again took the inside position. This time they left the gate together, but it was Fundin who got the best of the bend and he streaked away into a commanding lead. This time Craven had no chance and the Swedish star won comfortably, forcing the champion into a third-leg run-off. This was held at Southampton on 20 August and resulted in another 2-0 victory for Craven. Fundin had to wait another year before he finally wrested the title from Craven.

The Golden Helmet second leg however, was just an hors d'oeuvre before the main event that evening at Norwich, the Britannia Shield final second leg. It was to prove to be one of the best meetings ever witnessed at The Firs.

NORWICH SPEEDWAY

HOLT ROAD, NORWICH   'Phone : Norwich 46002

Souvenir OF THE

★ ★ ★ ★ ★ ★

"SUNDAY PICTORIAL"

GOLDEN HELMET

MATCH RACE CHAMPIONSHIP

P E T E R   C R A V E N

O V E   F U N D I N

AND THE

BRITANNIA CUP FINAL 1957

NORWICH v. BELLE VUE

OFFICIAL PROGRAMME
PRICE 1/-   N⁰ 1740

Programme cover.

Left: Ove Fundin and Peter Craven shake hands before meeting in the Golden Helmet Match Race Championship.

Opposite: Peter Craven in typically spectacular action.

There nearly was no 1957 speedway season. Following the Suez crisis, Britain was suffering from petrol rationing and a number of promoters were concerned that they would not be able to run a full season, partly because the supporters would not be able to get to the tracks and partly because of the problems the rationing would entail in honouring away fixtures. To meet these concerns, the control board decided to abandon the National Trophy altogether and not to start the National League until later in the year in the hope that by then the crisis would have eased. To start the season off, therefore, with a view to cutting travelling costs, a new regional competition was instituted called the Britannia Shield. This would consist of a Northern Section and a Southern Section, both run along league lines, with the winners of each section meeting to decide the destination of the shield. The winners of the Northern Section were Belle Vue and of the Southern Section Norwich. The final was to be a two-legged affair with the first leg taking place at Belle Vue on 20 July. Norwich took full advantage of the absence of two of the Belle Vue riders, Dick Fisher and Peter Williams, to surprise the speedway world by pulling off a 48–48 draw.

The second leg was delayed because there was a bus strike in Norfolk and did not take place until 7 August. Back on their home track, it seemed the Britannia Shield was Norwich's for the taking. For the Stars faithful it was a night not to be missed and

14,000 spectators arrived in the hope of watching their generally unfashionable team win a major trophy.

Whether the tension was getting to even that most experienced of campaigners, Norwich's captain Aub Lawson, or not, he started off proceedings in heat one by rearing at the start, leaving his teammate Phil Clarke to streak off into the lead. Lawson quickly managed to get his bike under control and pass the Belle Vue second string, Slant Payling. Meanwhile the Belle Vue captain, Ron Johnston, had set off in pursuit of Clarke, catching and passing him in a magnificent ride to share the points in the first race.

Heat two saw the two match race contenders up against each other, with Fundin once again getting the better of Craven. Behind them a ding-dong battle was taking place between Norwich's Geoff Pymar and Belle Vue's Peter Williams, with the Belle Vue man taking three laps before getting past Pymar, leaving the scores still level.

There were mixed fortunes for the Norwich pair at the start of the next heat as Bales shot off while Edwards got a very poor start. Duckworth and Fisher for Belle Vue chased after Bales and another gripping battle took place as Duckworth passed Bales who then repassed to take the lead again. This time he kept the lead and once more it was a shared heat.

There was another terrific tussle in heat four between Norwich's Wal Morton and Slant Payling, with Clarke only fractionally behind. Suddenly, Payling's bike slowed and Clarke and Belle Vue reserve Lew Grepp were able to nip through. At the same moment, Morton's bike failed completely and he had to pull off onto the centre green. Once again it was a 3–3.

At last Norwich made a breakthrough in heat five as Fundin romped home an easy winner. Behind him, however, there was more drama as Pymar was passed by a persistent and hard-riding Duckworth. Nevertheless it was a 4–2 to Norwich, which put them into the lead on the night and on aggregate.

Already the spectators that night had witnessed some of the most thrilling racing they had seen all season, with every race providing its share of passing and repassing, but heat six was to prove even better as a battle royal took place between Lawson and Craven. It was Lawson who gated first, hotly pursued by Craven and Clarke. For two laps Craven worried away at Lawson, poking his front wheel up in line with Lawson's rear wheel. Then, on the first bend of the third lap, he managed to get past, but Lawson was not finished and, coming into the fourth bend, he hit back, regaining the lead. There was pandemonium in the stadium as everyone was up on their feet cheering and urging their favourite on. Craven came back at Lawson while Clarke was also taking close order just inches behind Craven. Coming into the last bend it was still anyone's race, but Lawson just managed to hang on, as did Craven in second place. Another 4–2 to Norwich. It looked at last as though the hopes of those thousands of Norwich fans were about to be realised.

For the first time in the match the next heat saw no change in position as Johnston sped away from the tapes in front of Edwards and Bales, who then concentrated on team-riding Payling out of it as they had no chance of catching the flying Kiwi.

Heat eight saw another great race as Clarke took the lead in front of Duckworth with Lawson in third place. Lawson got past Duckworth, but Duckworth came back again, disposing of Lawson and tearing after Clarke, catching him on the last lap. Down the back straight the pair rode shoulder to shoulder, continuing this way as they entered the final bend but Clarke just had enough coming out onto the final straight to hold off the Belle Vue man's challenge. With Lawson in third spot it was another 4–2 to Norwich, and a clear six-point gap had opened up.

Craven won heat nine from the tapes with Edwards and Bales again team-riding, but this time they had no problems as Williams fell. 3–3.

With Fundin and Pymar away first in heat ten, the Swedish star tried to shepherd his teammate home, but Johnston managed to split the pair, leaving Fundin to go off as fast as he could. Unfortunately for him he overdid it and hit the fence, damaging his machine and forcing him to retire. With Johnston drawing away from Pymar it meant a 4–2 for Belle Vue and two points pulled back.

Pymar and Johnston were both out again in the next heat and it was a similar start as this time Lawson and Pymar got away, but once again Johnston was able to split the pair. A fine duel then took place between the New Zealander and Lawson as first Johnston got past Lawson, then Lawson repassed and finally, on the last lap, Johnston

Ron Johnston leads Aub Lawson in heat eleven with Bob Duckworth in third place.

regained the lead. Meanwhile, Duckworth also got past Pymar and chased hard after the leading pair. On the final bend with one last desperate lunge he managed to hurl his bike past Lawson and follow his captain home to make it a 5-1 to Belle Vue. After some of the best racing ever seen at The Firs, the scores were back to level with five heats to go.

It was nerve-wracking stuff for the Norwich faithful but still the drama continued as, in heat twelve, Clarke and Bales gated first and held their lead round the first bend, with Craven right behind them. On the second lap he managed to pass first Clarke and then, making a breakneck spurt round the outside, he disposed of Bales. Four heats to go and still all square.

Yet again the Norwich pair made the break in heat thirteen as Fundin and Morton entered the first-lap back straight in the lead. But not for long as Duckworth got past Morton. Behind them, Williams fell but managed to remount, though by now he was almost a lap behind. But fortune smiled on his brave effort as Morton's bike failed on the last bend and, although he tried to coast home, Williams just caught him on the line. Still the totals were level.

Heat fourteen also looked like being a 3-3 as Craven led from Pymar and Edwards, but Edwards suffered from a freak accident as his foot dug into the deep surface and he hurt his leg, forcing him to retire. The result, a 4-2 for Belle Vue, put them two points in front with just two heats left to race.

With Fundin out in the next heat, there was still hope for the Norwich fans, but it was Johnston all the way. Fundin dropped back to help Bales so that at least the Stars

Wal Morton, whose fall in the last heat secured victory for Belle Vue.

could get a 3-3 out of the heat but, on the last bend, Williams put in a supreme effort, taking Bales out and forcing his way past making it 4-2 for Belle Vue. With one heat to go the Aces were now four points in front, leaving Norwich needing a 5-1 to draw the match. The odds seemed to be very much on Norwich in the shape of Lawson and Edwards pulling it off, as both Fisher and Payling had had poor evenings, scoring just three points between them in eight rides. Unfortunately for Norwich, however, Edwards had not recovered sufficiently from the injury sustained in his previous heat and had to be replaced by Morton.

As the riders come out for the final heat the tension became almost unbearable; many Norwich fans looked away, unable to watch. The tapes went up to a deafening roar from the crowd, but before the riders even got to the back straight the match was all over as Morton fell on the first bend. Lawson took the chequered flag, but Belle Vue took the Britannia Shield.

It had been a magnificent evening's racing; the best seen at The Firs for many years and probably the best seen anywhere in the country in 1957. Both the racing and the match scores remained close all evening. Out of the sixteen heats only three contained no passing incidents; most contained passing and repassing. The Belle Vue heat-leader trio of Johnston, who scored a maximum fifteen, Craven and Duckworth were outstanding and even Fundin found it hard going against them.

Apart from the dominance of the Aces' heat leader trio, there was another factor at work in their victory, and one that was predicted in the match programme that night in an article by the *Speedway World* editor Peter Arnold, in which he said: 'Who will win? I'll say Norwich by about six. This much I know for sure: it's going to be tough going for either side and the winners will be worthy holders of the cup. The issue depends on the relative strengths of the reserve riders; the heats where they are concerned could well decide the match.' As it turned out, Norwich's reserve Wal Morton scored no points from three rides, while Belle Vue's reserve, Lew Grepp, scored three from two. This was almost the difference in the final scores.

Whoever was responsible for the final result, it has to be said that both teams put up a spirited performance and, although a tight match, not once were there any questionable tactics involved. Belle Vue rider Peter Williams remembers that no-one expected Belle Vue to win. 'The whole of the speedway world thought we'd lose, but they reckoned without Johnno [Ron Johnston]. Johnno was a hell of a good rider. He was good enough to win the World Championship if he'd been hungry enough but that night he really came good. His style was the complete opposite of Craven's; whereas Peter was a master of balance, Johnno was very upright. He always said there were three points of balance, your two hands on the handlebars and your foot on the ground; of course Peter very rarely put his foot on the ground. But between them that night they pulled off a great win – with the help of the rest of the team of course. I loved riding at Norwich, it was a large fast track which suited me. I still have the miniature shield we were each presented with that night.'

Ron Johnston recalls: 'I was captain of Belle Vue at the time. I liked riding at Norwich but they had a very strong team and every race was a hard one. Aub Lawson was always hard to beat; we had a lot of close races and I was lucky to win most of them. Ove Fundin was a very good rider of course and as a person we got on very well together. As for beating him twice that night, there were times when riding at some meetings I felt as though I could beat anybody, it didn't matter who they were, but I used to run a transport business at the time called Fletcher & Co. Ltd, which was the largest in the area, so I treated speedway as just part of the job though I did enjoy riding. I used to like team riding; a little trick I used to do when I wanted my teammate to hurry up would be to come underneath them with the throttle full on so as they could hear me. I learnt this trick from Jack Parker, who I partnered at Belle Vue at one time, and Ron Mason. I still have the shield we were presented with that night on my table at home.'

Ron Johnston, the Belle Vue captain, proudly displays the Britannia Shield.

Long-time Norwich fan Bryan Tungate remembers the match well. 'Yes I was there and yes I was pig-sick that we lost. The history of the match was that we had drawn 48-48 at Belle Vue in a match where Ove missed his first ride following bike trouble in his match races and Geoff Pymar had retired to promote at Exeter with Cyril Roger. Despite this we still held on to draw with Ove & Aub leading the way and the other team men supporting well. Geoff was back in the side for the second leg and both teams were at full strength. I personally feel that the Aces' match winner was Bob Duckworth, so often an unsung hero for the Aces. He strung together five second places, twice holding out Lawson, one in the vital heat eleven behind Johnston, which bought the scores to 33-33. The crowd was reported as 14,000 for the night and this was, I believe, the highest for the season. The next Norwich programme echoed many people's thoughts: "Speedway at its spectacular best; irrespective of the result, speedway was the winner." As I said I was really sick that we lost but I was used to that happening. After all it had happened before and would happen again. Norwich rode Ipswich the next week and won 69-27. This made up for the defeat in one go!'

With falling attendances in the mid to late 1950s causing many tracks to close, the meeting was a great advert for speedway at a time when it probably needed it the most.

7 August 1957: Norwich: Golden Helmet Match Race Championship

1: Peter Craven, Ove Fundin, 71.2 secs

2: Fundin, Craven, 72.0 secs

3: Fundin, Craven 71.8 secs

7 August 1957: Norwich v. Belle Vue: Britannia Shield Final Second Leg

NORWICH		1	2	3	4	5	Total
1	Aub Lawson (Capt.)	1	3	1	1	2	8
2	Phil Clarke	2	3	1	3	1	10
3	Ove Fundin	3	3	R	3	2	11
4	Geoff Pymar	0	1	2	0	2	5
5	Billy Bales	3	1	1	2	0	7
6	Harry Edwards	0	2	2	0	–	4
7	Wal Morton (Res.)	R	R	F	–	–	0

BELLE VUE		1	2	3	4	5	Total
1	Ron Johnston (Capt.)	3	3	3	3	3	15
2	Slant Payling	0	1	0	1	1	3
3	Peter Craven	2	2	3	3	3	13
4	Peter Williams	1	0	0	1	–	2
5	Dick Fisher	1	0	0	0	2	3
6	Bob Duckworth	2	2	2	2	2	10
7	Lew Grepp (Res.)	2	1	–	–	–	3

Heat 1: Johnston, Clarke, Lawson, Payling, 72.4 secs

Heat 2: Fundin, Craven, Williams, Pymar, 73.8 7 secs

Heat 3: Bales, Duckworth, Fisher, Edwards, 73.4 secs

Heat 4: Clarke, Grepp, Payling, Morton (e/f), 75.6 secs

Heat 5: Fundin, Duckworth, Pymar, Fisher, 74.6 secs

Heat 6: Lawson, Craven, Clarke, Williams, 73.6 secs

Heat 7: Johnston, Edwards, Bales, Payling, 73.0 secs

Heat 8: Clarke, Duckworth, Lawson, Fisher, 73.4 secs

Heat 9: Craven, Edwards, Bale, Williams, 73.6 secs

Heat 10: Johnston, Pymar, Payling, Fundin (e/f), 74.8 secs

Heat 11: Johnston, Duckworth, Lawson, Pymar, 73.8 secs

Heat 12: Craven, Bales, Clarke, Fisher, 73.6 secs

Heat 13: Fundin, Duckworth, Williams (f/rmtd), Morton (e/f), 73.4 secs

Heat 14: Craven, Pymar, Grepp, Edwards (r), 74.8 secs

Heat 15: Johnston, Fundin, Williams, Bales, 74.0 secs

Heat 16: Lawson, Fisher, Payling, Morton (f), 75.2 secs

10 June 1961

Edinburgh *v.* Rayleigh: Provincial League

The Provincial League was formed in 1960 and brought back several of the tracks that had closed down during the 1950s. Two of these were Edinburgh and Rayleigh. The Provincial League racing format was thirteen heats. Each rider had four scheduled rides except for the reserve, who was programmed to ride only in heats three and eight. There was no nominated riders heat but heat thirteen always had the top men out with the numbers one and three from each team meeting.

On 10 June 1961 Edinburgh took on Rayleigh in a league match. The Rayleigh Rockets were a southern-based English powerhouse team with three superb heat leaders in Reg Reeves, Stan Stevens and Harry Edwards. The previous season, 1960, the inaugural season of the Provincial League, they had inflicted the biggest home defeat of the season on the Edinburgh Monarchs by 27-45 and had taken the league championship.

In the style befitting the league champions, the Rayleigh team arrived in Edinburgh on board The Flying Scotsman. Rayleigh reserve that night, Terry Stone, remembers that they used to park their vans in the road next to King's Cross Station ('there were no yellow lines in those days'), wheel their bikes onto the train and then be met at Edinburgh's Waverley Station by the Edinburgh riders in their vans who gave them and their bikes a lift to the stadium, where they were greeted by a smaller-than-usual crowd of Monarchs supporters who had braved the rain eagerly anticipating an exciting evening's racing, hoping against hope that their three heat leaders, Doug Templeton, George Hunter and Dick Campbell, could prove a match for the champions' celebrated trio.

As the match began these hopes looked doomed to disappointment as, sure enough, on their first appearance, the Rayleigh top three took their respective heats convincingly. All was not quite lost, however, as the Monarchs' second strings managed to pack the minor places and, with Wayne Briggs taking the reserves' heat (heat three), the scores after four heats were all level at 12-12. Edinburgh's breakthrough came in heat five as their captain, Doug Templeton, managed to pin Stevens back into second place with the result that the home side took a 4-2 and moved into a two-point lead. Edwards and Reeves continued their winning ways in heats six and seven, but once again the Monarchs packed the minor placings so that at the halfway stage, heat seven, Edinburgh still held on to their slender two-point lead 22-20. With none of the Rayleigh stars out in heat eight, Edinburgh felt this had to be their big chance to press home their advantage, but it was not to be as Jimmy Tannock suffered an engine failure, leaving the Rockets' Bob Thomas to lead home Briggs and the scores were back to level at 24 each. This was disastrous for Edinburgh as heat eight was one of the only two heats that did not include one of the Rayleigh heat leaders and therefore one of the only two they could reasonably hope to win.

EDINBURGH Speedway

OFFICIAL PROGRAMME

SATURDAY, 10th JUNE 1961, at 7.15 p.m.
PROVINCIAL LEAGUE

MONARCHS v RAYLEIGH

Control Board Licence No. 61/12.   A.C.U. Permit No. 591

Strictly no Betting

6 D

GEORGE HUNTER—Cradley had him 'taped'   Photo by Edinburgh Evening Dispatch

Programme cover.

The 1961 Edinburgh team. From left to right, back row: Alf Wells, Doug Templeton, Willie Templeton, Ian Hoskins (Promoter). Front row: Jimmy Tannock, Wayne Briggs, George Hunter, Dick Campbell.

Heat nine went the way of most of the previous heats, finishing as a 3-3, with Edwards winning for Rayleigh. Once again, however, it was to be Stevens who proved to be the Rockets' weak link as, in heat ten, Dick Campbell headed him home and with Alf Wells taking third place Edinburgh were back in the lead 31-29. With Reeves out twice and Edwards once in the last three heats the match was building to a nail-biting climax. Reeves duly won heat eleven and another 3-3 was the result.

Heat twelve saw Edwards beat Campbell, who was riding one of five different bikes that night. But with Alf Wells suffering engine problems, Terry Stone was able to capitalise and a 4-2 for Rayleigh levelled the scores with just one heat to go.

The final and deciding heat turned out to be one of those races that will never be forgotten by those who were fortunate to be in the crowd that Saturday night. Reg Reeves was off gate one, George Hunter was off gate two, Stan Stevens was off gate three and Doug Templeton was off gate four. Reeves went into the race undefeated while Hunter had had three thirds and Templeton had lost to Reeves. It looked a certain win for Rayleigh or, at the very worst for them, if Templeton and Hunter could defeat Rayleigh's heat leader weak link that night, Stevens, a draw.

When the tapes went up it was a fairly even break with Reeves showing slightly ahead, but he drifted wide and George Hunter was through. Stan Stevens was in third place with Doug Templeton at the back. On the second lap Hunter pinned Reeves on the curve riding the white line. He made a slight wobble that put Reeves off and gave him a bit of breathing space just when it seemed he must be passed. Templeton, however, was still stuck at the back. Third lap – no change and a draw looked a distinct possibility if Hunter could just keep it going. But there was no need for Edinburgh fans to worry on that score as Hunter rode an immaculate last lap to sail home in first place. The action now switched to the back as Templeton, on the third bend of the last lap, rode straight up the banking at the top of the bend then cut back hard and caught Stevens with an amazing passing movement just before crossing the line. What a finish!

A 4-2 to the Monarchs and a last-gasp victory. The crowd went wild and the cheers could be heard all over Edinburgh.

Recalling the match, Edinburgh supporter Dennis Wallace said: 'This was a match never to be forgotten. I wish they could all be like that – you'd never be able to get all the crowd in! I can still remember a lot of that meeting, particularly heat thirteen, which will live with me forever because it was just as good as seeing your team score the winning goal in the cup final. I was just a slip of a lad at the time but I remember jumping about the terracing hugging people to share in the joy of the moment. What do I remember about that match? Well I remember that it had rained up till 6 p.m. that Saturday night so the crowd was a bit smaller than usual. I was just a teenager at the time and fanatical about speedway. I persuaded my cousin to go to Old Meadowbank for the match with me although he seldom went to speedway matches until after this one! Having lost to the Rayleigh Rockets 27-45 at home in 1960 we expected to get well beaten again. Rayleigh had won the Provincial League in 1960, after which some of their team went down to Exeter to form the Exeter Falcons. As a result they were not as strong as they had been the previous year but still looked more than capable of seeing off the Monarchs. Up until that point Edinburgh had an unbeaten home record in the league, having beaten Wolverhampton, Middlesbrough,

George Hunter, winner of the final heat for Edinburgh.

Doug Templeton, Edinburgh's captain.

Sheffield, Plymouth and Cradley Heath. Right from the start my guts were churning as the first four heats were all shared. The main problem for the Edinburgh riders was trying to match the Rayleigh big guns of Reg Reeves, Stan Stevens and Harry Edwards. Heat three was a big disappointment since, with only the Rayleigh two and seven to beat, Willie Templeton finished last behind Wayne Briggs, Roy Craighead and Terry Stone. That would be the last time until heat eight that Rayleigh would race a heat without one of their big three. A 4-2 in heat five gave us all hope but we really felt that we needed to get an advantage from heat eight against the Rayleigh four and seven. Two more drawn heats and we reached that fateful heat. Disaster! Jimmy Tannock suffered an engine failure (although he was at the back at the time) and we lost it 2-4 with Bob Thomas winning it for the only points he scored all night and Terry Stone finishing third behind Wayne Briggs. That looked to be it since Rayleigh were now back on level terms at 24-24 with heat leaders in each of the last five heats. Dick Campbell got the better of Stan Stevens though in heat ten and the excitement rose as we took a 4-2 to hit the front again, only to lose our two-point advantage when Dick Campbell disappointingly could only finish second to Harry Edwards, with Alf Wells having an engine failure, resulting in a 2-4 to Rayleigh and a 36-36 scoreline going into the last heat. You must have experienced that sinking feeling of desperate hope, expecting the worst but hoping for a miracle in the last heat. Well, we got the miracle finish. What more can I say?'

In the match programme the following week, promoter Ian Hoskins wrote: 'We have seen some thrilling meetings over the past two seasons at Edinburgh, but rarely have we had one to compare with the Rayleigh match of last Saturday. I had resigned myself to the prospect of possible defeat with a draw as the only consolation to look forward to when the boys lined up for heat thirteen. The points were level 36–36 and Doug Templeton and George Hunter had won only one race between them in their previous rides. They faced the unbeaten Reg Reeves and the hard-riding Stan Stevens of Rayleigh. The Rayleigh promoter, Wally Mawdsley, had a grin as big as a slice of melon and who could blame him? Up went the tapes and the four machines broke level. Out of the first bend came Reg Reeves, slightly ahead of George Hunter. Wally Mawdsley had already begun a war dance. Then came the second bend. Reeves drifted wide and George Hunter was through. How the crowd roared! With George away in front, Reeves and Stevens tried to shut out Dougie into fourth place. For over two laps he battled and then Stevens left a gap. Before you could say "Bob's your uncle" big Dougie was through and there wasn't a still voice in the entire stadium. The 4–2 victory won the match for Monarchs and our unbeaten home record had been preserved for another week.'

Dennis Wallace continues: 'It was Hoskins at his best. What a promoter and showman! Incidentally Rayleigh returned to Old Meadowbank in the second round

Rayleigh's Reg Reeves (left) battles it out with Doug Templeton.

of the sixteen-heat KO Cup four weeks later on 8 July 1961 and Edinburgh beat them again, this time 49-47, in a match where they trailed until heat thirteen. When my cousin and I left the stadium (after the second half, which consisted of a rider of the night trophy won by Reg Reeves from Harry Edwards and Doug Templeton) we were walking on cloud nine in a state of schoolboy euphoria!'

Immediately after the meeting, Rayleigh's maximum man Harry Edwards said: 'Usually the tracks I have to ride on are so rough I get tired. Tonight I could have raced forever. It is the best track I've met this season.'

Two of the Edinburgh riders later commented on the match. George Hunter said he was delighted to win heat thirteen against Rayleigh for a special reason: 'I felt pretty bad about stalling my motor in the last race at Cradley Heath the Saturday before. I'm glad I was able to make up for it.'

Dick Campbell, who had been having mechanical problems prior to the match, said: 'I rode five different bikes during the Rayleigh meeting. My own bike lost its power and we couldn't find the reason.'

Ian Hoskins recalls: 'The second year I ran the Monarchs, both Hunter and Dougie [Templeton] were coming into their own. This was obviously a great breakthrough for the team at the time. I can remember having strong words with both Hunter and Templeton in the pits prior to the final heat. The way they rode they must have taken some notice of me! The great thing about that era in speedway was that the outcome of meetings were rarely predictable in advance.'

Dick Campbell, riding one of the five machines he had to call in to action for the meeting.

Harry Edwards scored a maximum for Rayleigh.

On the Rayleigh side, Stan Stevens says he can remember two things about the match in particular: 'The first is Harry Edwards telling the younger Rayleigh riders in the dressing room before the start that the way to ride Edinburgh was just to go full throttle round the outside. He then proceeded to put this into practice and he just went hell for leather round the boards. As it happens, he must have been right because he was the only unbeaten rider all night. But the other thing that I can still recall vividly was that last heat. I thought I was holding Templeton, but as I rode in to the last bend on the fourth lap I could see the whole crowd in the main stand rise to their feet as one and that was when I realised that Doug had got me with that amazing manoeuvre when he cut through on the inside of me.'

Terry Stone remembers that, even though the Rayleigh team returned on the prestigious Flying Scotsman, the journey home was not a very happy one: 'Stan Collis [the Rayleigh manager] wanted to hold a postmortem and talked about the meeting all the way back and what had gone wrong. We just wanted him to shut up so we could get some sleep. We were all laid out across the seats but he wouldn't stop talking!'

Meanwhile, back in Edinburgh, the celebrations were continuing...

10 June 1961: Edinburgh v. Rayleigh: Provincial League

EDINBURGH		1	2	3	4	Total
1	Doug Templeton (Capt.)	2	3	2	1	8
2	Willie Templeton	1	0	1	1	3
3	George Hunter	1	1	1	3	6
4	Jimmy Tannock	2	2	R	2	6
5	Dick Campbell	2	2	3	2	9
6	Alf Wells (Res.)	1	1	1	R	3
7	Wayne Briggs (Res.)	3	2	–	–	5

RAYLEIGH		1	2	3	4	Total
1	Reg Reeves (Capt.)	3	3	3	2	11
2	Roy Craighead	0	2	0	0	2
3	Stan Stevens	3	2	2	0	7
4	Bob Thomas	0	0	3	0	3
5	Harry Edwards	3	3	3	3	12
6	Pete Sampson (Res.)	0	0	0	–	0
7	Terry Stone (Res.)	1	1	1	–	3

Heat 1: Reeves, D. Templeton, W. Templeton, Craighead, 70.8 secs

Heat 2: Stevens, Tannock, Hunter, Thomas, 71.2 secs

Heat 3: Briggs, Craighead, Stone, W. Templeton, 78.6 secs

Heat 4: Edwards, Campbell, Wells, Sampson, 70.2 secs

Heat 5: D. Templeton, Stevens, W. Templeton, Thomas, 71.4 secs

Heat 6: Edwards, Tannock, Hunter, Sampson, 71.0 secs

Heat 7: Reeves, Campbell, Wells, Craighead, 70.8 secs

Heat 8: Thomas, Briggs, Stone, Tannock (e/f), 73.0 secs

Heat 9: Edwards, D. Templeton, W. Templeton, Sampson, 71.0 secs

Heat 10: Campbell, Stevens, Wells, Thomas, 70.4 secs

Heat 11: Reeves, Tannock, Hunter, Craighead, 70.6 secs

Heat 12: Edwards, Campbell, Stone, Wells (e/f), 71.0 secs

Heat 13: Hunter, Reeves, D. Templeton, Stevens, 71.4 secs

14 August 1965

Wimbledon *v.* West Ham: Knock Out Cup Quarter-Final Replay

In 1960, a new Knock-Out Cup competition had been introduced by the Provincial League. Until then all cup events, such as the National Trophy and the London Cup, had always been held over two legs to even out home track advantage. The new cup was based on football's FA Cup, with the result being decided on just one match. As in football, it was the luck of the draw which team got the home tie. In 1961 the National League also adopted this format so that in 1965, when the new British League was formed from the old National and Provincial Leagues, it was natural that the Knock-Out Cup should continue. One of the quarter-final matches that year saw West Ham drawn at home to Wimbledon. The match was held on 3 August. Before the tie, the two teams appeared to be evenly matched and so it proved. With one heat to go the scores were level at 45-45. The atmosphere was tense as the two London rivals came out for the last heat knowing that whoever got the advantage would march on to the semi-finals. The riders were on edge and this was reflected in the fact that there were two faulty starts. As the riders finally got away at the third time of asking it was the Wimbledon pair, Olle Nygren and Reg Luckhurst, who took an early lead over Brian Leonard and Norman Hunter. It looked all over for the Hammers when, suddenly, Luckhurst's engine blew up resulting in a 3-3 and a tied match at 48-48.

The replay was arranged for Saturday 14 August at Plough Lane. Having drawn at West Ham, Wimbledon looked a good bet to take the tie on their own track. But there was even worse news for West Ham as their top rider, Sverre Harrfeldt, ranked at number nine in the world, had been injured the previous evening at Hackney and was unable to take part and their third heat leader, Norman Hunter, was also unable to ride as it was his wedding day! There were no guests, so the Hammers had to resort to filling the places of two heat leaders with two novices: Tony Clarke, who was making his team debut, and Wimbledon junior Geoff Hughes. The position was slightly evened up by the fact that Wimbledon had also lost one of their heat leaders, Trevor Hedge, through injury. Nevertheless, with only one recognised heat leader riding, no-one, not even the West Ham supporters present that afternoon, gave the Hammers much hope.

The first heat saw the two captains in opposition as Wimbledon's Olle Nygren, along with his partner Jim Tebby, took on Ken McKinlay and his partner Reg Trott. Giving the Hammers' faithful something to cheer about, Ken McKinlay managed to get the better of Nygren and the first heat resulted in a 3-3. Two more 3-3s followed. Nygren and McKinlay met once again in heat four; this time Nygren proved too good for McKinlay as Wimbledon took their expected lead with a 4-2. The following heat saw Luckhurst win but again West Ham filled the minor placings with Malcolm Simmons, the Hammers' young second string, taking second place.

WIMBLEDON
SPEEDWAY

SATURDAY 14th AUGUST, 1965

OFFICIAL PROGRAMME NINEPENCE

Programme cover.

West Ham's teenage hero Malcolm Simmons.

Heat six and it looked at last as though Wimbledon's superiority was about to become clear as Olle Nygren, along with the experienced Jim Tebby, took a 5-1 against West Ham's newcomer Tony Clarke and second string Brian Leonard. The lack of two heat leaders looked as though it was now beginning to tell. However, as West Ham were six points in arrears it meant they could use a tactical substitute and their team manager for the night, Dave Lanning, wasted no time in bringing in Ken McKinlay for reserve Ray Wickett in the very next heat. The line-up for heat seven was therefore Bob Dugard and Keith Whipp for the Dons, Malcolm Simmons and Ken McKinlay for the Hammers. The young Simmons shot away from the gate with McKinlay behind him and that's how the heat finished. A 5-1 for West Ham and four points pulled back. Amazingly, Simmons' time of 66.2 secs was the fastest of the night. The next heat saw McKinlay out again, this time in a scheduled ride, with old campaigner Reg Trott lining up against Reg Luckhurst and reserve Mike Coomber. Some brilliant team riding by McKinlay and Trott kept Luckhurst behind them and, with Coomber falling, it meant another 5-1 to the Hammers who, unbelievably, at the halfway stage, now found themselves with a two-point lead.

Another 3-3 in heat nine kept the Hammers in front. With Nygren and Tebby lined up against Simmons and Wickett in heat ten it looked as though the Dons would edge back into the lead but, once again, Simmons rose to the occasion and beat Nygren in the second-fastest time of the night. Heat eleven saw Luckhurst and Coomber up against West Ham's most inexperienced pairing of Clarke and Leonard, but it was Leonard who gated first. To the excited cheers of the Hammers' supporters, Leonard managed to hold off Luckhurst for over three laps. Luckhurst tried everything he knew to get by, finally making it on the fourth bend of the fourth lap. Nevertheless it was another 3-3 and West Ham were still holding on to their slender lead.

Heat twelve saw another astonishing turn of events as Dugard fell, bringing down Trott and Whipp with him, and was excluded from the rerun. It was a simple matter for McKinlay and Trott to defeat Whipp and take a 5-1. It was now West Ham who were six points up as they went into heat thirteen leading 39–33. It was now Wimbledon who used a tactical substitute as they brought in Nygren for reserve John Edwards. As the tapes rose it looked as though the substitution would have its desired effect as Nygren flew into an early lead. Behind him, Malcolm Simmons was having a tremendous tussle with Reg Luckhurst, the only man to have beaten him so far. Ray Wickett was tailed-off last. By lap three, Simmons had finally shaken off Luckhurst and went off in hot pursuit of the Wimbledon captain, finally catching him on the third bend of the last lap. At this point, Nygren made a crucial error and drifted wide, letting the young Hammer by on the inside. As they came round the apex of the bend, Simmons was just inches in front, but Nygren seemed to have the extra speed as they came out of the bend onto the final straight, but, amazingly, Simmons held his line and seemed to get some extra grip, propelling him across the line in first place. For the second time that night Simmons had beaten Nygren, leaving West Ham still six points in front.

The 1965 West Ham full-strength team. From left to right: Reg Trott, Ken McKinlay, Norman Hunter, Dave Lanning (Press and Publicity Officer), Brian Leonard, Malcolm Simmons, Sverre Harrfeldt, Ted Ede.

With just three heats to go time was running out for Wimbledon and the Hammers' impossible task suddenly looked possible. However, a Nygren and Dugard 5-1 over Trott and Leonard put them back in with a chance and when, in heat fifteen, Tebby and Coomber pulled off a 4-2 against Clarke and Hughes, the scores, with one heat left, were once again level.

The line-up for that final heat saw Keith Whipp and Reg Luckhurst for Wimbledon against Ken McKinlay and West Ham's new hero Malcolm Simmons. The tension around the stadium was palpable. Everyone was holding their breath. The riders from both teams came out onto the centre green to urge their colleagues on. A match that, at the beginning of the afternoon, had seemed likely to be very one-sided had now come down to a last-heat decider, just like the first leg.

To some extent the final race as a race was a bit of a disappointment as Simmons flew off from the start and never looked to be in any danger, and with McKinlay settling for a steady third place behind Luckhurst, the match was won by West Ham by 49 points to 47. The small band of Hammers' supporters who had made the trip across London could not believe what had happened. The hero of the hour was the nineteen-year-old Malcolm Simmons. He had beaten the Wimbledon captain, Olle Nygren, normally nigh on unbeatable on his own Plough Lane track, twice and had set the three fastest times of the night. In fact he still wasn't finished. In the second-half scratch race event, the Cheer Leaders' Trophy, he won the first heat, beating McKinlay, Luckhurst and Dugard and then went on to win the final, once again beating Nygren. As if that wasn't bad enough for the Dons' fans, a special Handicap race was held with Simmons starting off twenty yards, Nygren off ten and Trott, Leonard and Tebby off scratch. Yet again, Simmons got the better of Nygren, even with his handicap.

In the West Ham programme the following week, manager Tommy Price wrote: '…our lads rose magnificently to the occasion… It was certainly my most emotional moment in speedway since winning the World Championship, and everyone in the Plough Lane Stadium was thrilled to the core by speedway racing at its glorious best. It's difficult to single out anyone for special attention, but young Malcolm's fourteen points finally heralded the lad's arrival as a star, and a future champion if ever there was one.'

That night proved to be a turning point both for West Ham's season and Malcolm Simmons' career. The scale of his achievement that afternoon should not be underestimated. At the start of the meeting he was a nineteen-year-old second string who had had a reasonable season, scoring at an average of between five and six points per match and shown promise of good things to come, but had done nothing to show that he could beat the best. And yet here he was beating the likes of Nygren and Luckhurst on their own track. In the end-of-season ratings produced by a panel of experts from around the world on behalf of the authoritative speedway journal the *Speedway Star and News*, Nygren was ranked number sixteen in the world and Luckhurst number twenty-one. From that afternoon on there was no looking back for Simmons and, in effect, he became West Ham's fourth heat leader with the result that the Hammers did not lose another official fixture all season, sweeping to victory in the first-ever British League, the Knock-Out Cup and the London Cup.

West Ham's captain and inspiration, Ken McKinlay.

Simmons himself, of course, went on to become one of Great Britain's greatest ever riders; runner-up in the 1976 World Championship, World Pairs Champion in 1976, 1977 and 1978, World Team Champion in 1973, 1974, 1975 and 1977 and British Champion in 1976. He was capped 80 times for England, 7 times for the British Lions (touring Australia), 5 times for Great Britain and 4 times for the Rest of the World.

Recalling the match, Malcolm Simmons said that the West Ham team had gone to the meeting thinking they would get thrashed but somehow the whole team had risen to the occasion. He went on to say: 'It was the first good meeting I ever had for West Ham. I just came good on the night. I liked the Wimbledon track anyway, but I had also been given a tip by Reg Luckhurst on how to beat Nygren. Reg told me "if you don't trap in front of him, just follow him closely as he'll eventually go wide and you'll be able to get through on the inside." And that's exactly what happened. In one race I outgated him, but in the other he beat me out of the start so I just hung on and eventually, on the last lap, he went wide and I nipped through on the inside, so Reg's advice paid off. Although it was my best performance I have to say that the whole team did better than expected; we wouldn't have just won it on my score. We were over the moon afterwards. It was an unbelievable result to go to Wimbledon and win without Harrfeldt and Hunter and, of course, we never looked back for the rest of the season. I still remember that meeting as one of my best ever.'

Reg Trott also had good reason to remember the meeting: 'It was a bit special. At the beginning of the season Bob Dugard was at West Ham but not doing very well. He wanted to transfer to Wimbledon. Strings were pulled and they swapped me for Bob. I suppose I was out to show Wimbledon that they had made a mistake and I think I had a terrific season at West Ham as we won everything going that year. When we went to Wimbledon that afternoon we knew we were going to have a hard time but, as we know now, it was the day Malcolm came good and we cracked it. We had a team talk before the match from Dave Lanning, who was acting as team manager, and our captain Ken McKinlay, who both tried to encourage us to do our best. We knew we were up against it without Norman and Sverre, but it turned out great. I remember one race [heat twelve] I was behind Bob Dugard and he came down. I managed to put my bike down and just missed him. Bob came over and thanked me and we've been pals ever since.'

For Dave Lanning, who was acting as team manager for the match, it was a day he would never forget: 'Norman Hunter had chosen that day to get married because, of course, originally there was no speedway fixture but, as it turned out, it was the only day we could fit the replay in. Because we were going as guests to the wedding anyway, Ken [McKinlay] and I were deputed by Tommy Price to try and persuade Norman to leave the reception and come and ride for us. We did our best. We told Norman that he could still be back home in time for his wedding night but his bride, Janet, said there was no way she was letting him go and ride on their wedding day. We were there till about 6:30 trying to talk them into it but, in the end, we had to leave without him. When we arrived at the stadium, we just had time to hold a quick team talk. I just said that people are saying there is no way we can win tonight, it's impossible and that we'll be lucky to get twenty-five points. But I'm telling you you can win tonight, now just go out there and go for it. With both Hunter and Harrfeldt out I had to quickly rearrange the team and the riding order. I put in Tony Clarke at number three. He was absolutely stunned. He hadn't expected to get a ride, let alone ride at number three, but he rode his heart out and the four points he scored made all the difference to the final result. Of course that wasn't the only reason we won. There were several other factors, the most important being Malcolm Simmons. He had been steadily improving but that night marked his arrival in the big time. After coming second in his first ride, no-one saw him for dust all night. In truth, Simmons was a brilliant rider but had been having trouble with his bike all season. After the meeting, he said to me: "I don't know what's happened to my bike, but it's flying tonight." The funny thing was he didn't dare touch it after that; he didn't even clean it for fear of upsetting whatever it was he'd managed to get right! Ken was his usual cagey self and rode well for his thirteen points. Brian [Leonard], always a useful second string, popped up and excelled himself. It was a stunning team performance. No-one believed we could go there and win without two heat leaders. The loss of Harrfeldt had been an especially difficult blow as he had ridden for Wimbledon the year before and was an acknowledged Plough Lane specialist. It was just a remarkable victory and certainly rates in my mind as one of the classic team performances of all time.'

Wimbledon captain Olle Nygren.

One of the West Ham supporters who was there that afternoon, John Hill, said: 'I can still remember that match as if it was yesterday. In fact I can remember it better than matches I saw last season. It was just such an amazing afternoon. I went along there with a few other Hammers' supporters expecting a reasonable match but when it was announced just before the meeting started that neither Harrfeldt nor Hunter would be taking part we seriously considered going home. The Wimbledon supporters around us were saying things like "You'll be lucky if you get twenty points" and "This is going to be the biggest thrashing of all time." Of course we gave back as good as we got but in our hearts we felt they could well be right. We were given some hope as the match started but when we went six points behind we felt it was all over. Then suddenly there was this rider called Malcolm Simmons, who we had seen rise from the ranks of a second-halfer at West Ham to a reasonable second string but no more, taking on and beating the likes of Olle Nygren and Reg Luckhurst on their own track in the fastest times of the night. He was just phenomenal. One thing I do remember well is the way the Wimbledon fans fell more and more silent as the match progressed, although it was still tense right until the end and the match wasn't decided until the last heat. Of course, Malcolm couldn't win the match on his own and the others, particularly Ken McKinlay and Brian Leonard, played their part as well, Ken with his team riding and Brian also, like Malcolm, riding above himself.'

Although Simmons went onto bigger and better things, this was the best it ever got for the Hammers as a team. After winning everything in sight in 1965 they went into a permanent decline, coming one from last in the British League in 1969 and 1970, finally going one worse by finishing bottom in 1971. It was too much for the promotion and the fans and, at the end of that season, the Hammers withdrew from the league.

14 August 1965: Wimbledon *v.* West Ham: Knock-Out Cup Quarter-Final Replay

WIMBLEDON		1	2	3	4	5	6	Total
1	Olle Nygren (Capt.)	2	3	3	2	2	2	14
2	Jim Tebby	1	3	2	1	3	–	10
3	Bobby Dugard	3	1	1	X	3	–	8
4	Keith Whipp	0	0	1	1	0	–	2
5	Reg Luckhurst	3	1	3	1	2	–	10
6	John Edwards (Res.)	F	0	–	–	–	–	0
7	Mike Coomber (Res.)	F	F	2	F	1	–	3

WEST HAM		1	2	3	4	5	6	Total
1	Ken McKinlay (Capt.)	3	2	2	2	3	1	13
2	Reg Trott	0	2	3	2	0	–	7
3	Tony Clarke	1	0	0	1	2	–	4
4	Brian Leonard	2	1	3	2	1	–	9
5	Malcolm Simmons	2	3	3	3	3	–	14
6	Ray Wickett (Res.)	1	0	0	–	–	–	1
7	Geoff Hughes (Res.)	1	0	0	–	–	–	1

Heat 1: McKinlay, Nygren, Tebby, Trott, 67.0 secs

Heat 2: Dugard, Leonard, Clarke, Whipp, 69.8 secs

Heat 3: Tebby, Trott, Hughes, Coomber (f), 68.8 secs

Heat 4: Nygren, McKinlay, Dugard, Clarke, 67.2 secs

Heat 5: Luckhurst, Simmons, Wickett, Edwards (f), 67.4

Heat 6: Nygren, Tebby, Leonard, Clarke, 69.0 secs

Heat 7: Simmons, McKinlay, Dugard, Whipp, 66.2 secs

Heat 8: Trott, McKinlay, Luckhurst, Coomber (f), 68.2 secs

Heat 9: Leonard, Coomber, Whipp, Hughes, 68.0 secs

Heat 10: Simmons, Nygren, Tebby, Wickett, 66.4 secs

Heat 11: Luckhurst, Leonard, Clarke, Coomber (f), 67.8 secs

Heat 12 (Rerun): McKinlay, Trott, Whipp, Dugard (f/exc), 70.8 secs

Heat 13: Simmons, Nygren, Luckhurst, Wickett, 66.6 secs

Heat 14: Dugard, Nygren, Leonard, Trott, 70.2 secs

Heat 15: Tebby, Clarke, Coomber, Hughes, 70.8 secs

Heat 16: Simmons, Luckhurst, McKinlay, Whipp, 67.2 secs

15 July 1973: Wembley

England *v.* Sweden, *Daily Mirror* International Tournament Final

The summer of 1973 saw British speedway host the *Daily Mirror* International Tournament. It was a competition that captured the imagination of the general public and the national media alike.

Seven international teams containing the world's greatest riders were gathered for a mini-league format, which climaxed with a one-off final at Wembley Stadium. It was the nearest the sport had ever come, or indeed ever has, to a football-style World Cup event. Hosts England were joined by Australia, the USSR, Sweden, Poland, New Zealand and a combined Norway/Denmark side for the festival of world-class action that took in eighteen British tracks in nineteen days. Fans flocked to the meetings in their droves and television and newspapers alike offered the tournament enormous amounts of coverage – little wonder, with shale superstars such as Ivan Mauger, Ole Olsen, Ronnie Moore, Zenon Plech, Peter Collins, Ray Wilson, Anders Michanek and Barry Briggs all playing starring roles.

England began as tournament favourites but Sweden, with the powerful Michanek, 1972 world number two Bernt Persson, and former world number three Soren Sjosten in their squad, were also obvious contenders. As too were New Zealand, who had reigning world champion Mauger, Briggs and Moore in their ranks. The latter two may have been marginally past their prime but, as a trio, they still held an incredible nine World Individual Championships up to that point. No other side in the tournament could boast that sort of pedigree. Denmark/Norway had the classy 1971 world champion Ole Olsen and the talented Dag Lovaas and Reider Eide. The Aussies had a solid look about them and the Poles and Russians were unpredictable but never to be underestimated.

The tournament began inauspiciously enough with two rain-offs, namely the England *v.* New Zealand and Australia *v.* Norway/Denmark clashes scheduled for Leicester and Coventry respectively. So the first match to actually take place was the England *v.* Sweden match at Sheffield. A thrilling encounter ensued at the pacy Owlerton bowl, which went down to a last-heat decider that did not disappoint. England's exciting new star Collins and the wily Yorkshireman Eric Boocock faced Michanek and the talented Tommy Jansson with the scores locked at 36-36. The Swedes established an early advantage and were set for a match winning 4-2 with Michanek leading from Collins, Jansson and Boocock in that order. But on the last lap, the English duo executed simultaneous overtaking manoeuvres around the outside to swing the scores in their favour and give England a 40-38 victory that almost brought the house down. The meeting set the touch paper alight for the tournament, for the England-Sweden rivalry and, in particular, for the rivalry between Collins and Michanek. With confidence running high, England marched through the rest of their

Daily Mirror International Speedway Tournament Final Plus Great Britain v The Rest of the World Wembley Stadium Saturday 14 July 1973 Official Programme 15p

Programme cover.

Left: England hero Peter Collins.

Opposite: Swedish giant Anders Michanek.

league matches, beating Norway/Denmark, USSR, Poland and Australia without too much difficulty.

Sweden suffered another two-point reverse, this time at the hands of Australia, but were otherwise unbeaten. The final league standings left England, New Zealand, Sweden and Australia in the semi-finals.

The youthful England line-up put the experienced New Zealand to the sword at Belle Vue 48-30 to ease through to the final. Meanwhile, at Coventry, Sweden gained gleeful revenge on Australia with a thumping 51-27 victory. However, the Swedes suffered a blow with the loss of their skipper, Hackney's Bengt Jansson, who injured his knee in a clash with Garry Middleton to rule him out of the final. But this did not stop the Hackney rider indulging in a bit of verbal jousting with his English counterpart, Ray Wilson of Leicester, before the big night. 'We feel it is about time Sweden got back to the top position in speedway. We must have more top riders now than for some years. Most of our riders are quite confident. We have all had at least some success in one or other of the meetings: Michanek broke the track record at Hackney and (Christer) Lofqvist at Swindon and such things are good for confidence.' Wilson replied: 'We're not short on confidence ourselves – especially with boys like Peter Collins doing so well. He really has been one of the tremendous successes of the tournament.'

However, as the bikes rolled into a packed Empire Stadium on Saturday 15 July, the time for talking was done and the stage was set for a mouthwatering confrontation.

England fielded a powerful looking septet of Wilson, Collins, Boocock, Martin Ashby, John Louis, Malcolm Simmons and Terry Betts. Sweden, despite the loss of skipper Jansson, still had a mighty line-up to call upon, consisting of Michanek, Persson, Sjosten, Tommy Jansson, Christer Lofqvist, Hasse Holmqvist and Olle Nygren.

Heat one saw England make their intentions clear from the off. Wilson made a clean start and rode an immaculate inside line to lead throughout from a battling Lofqvist. Ashby, meanwhile, gave Holmqvist a huge shove as he moved inside him on lap one to give the home country an early advantage. The lead was doubled in heat two when a great start from Simmons saw him lead Jansson, Betts and Nygren to the flag. Heat three brought Persson to the start line. The previous year the Cradley Heath rider had almost won the World final on the same track, narrowly losing a run-off to Mauger for the title. Once again, he proved his liking for the hallowed shale as he streaked to a tapes-to-flag victory. Behind him the English duo of Collins and Louis never really sorted out who was going to challenge the dashing Swede and consequently were forced to settle for a 3-3.

The next race saw the emergence of Sweden's star man Anders Michanek and he looked quite superb, leaving the rest of the field for dead as he hurtled to a clear victory of around thirty lengths. Behind him, Simmons spent three laps harassing Jansson before finally going around him as they entered the final lap to ensure England still held a precious, if slender, two-point lead.

The next heat was drawn, with Collins holding off the pesky attentions of Lofqvist and Louis surprisingly making little impression on Holmqvist for third. Michanek oozed class in heat six as he scorched clear of the Englishmen and, despite his best efforts, Wilson simply could not get near him. But with a sadly out-of-touch Nygren, standing in as skipper for the night, tailed off at the back, it was another drawn heat.

Sweden cancelled out England's advantage in heat seven as Persson and Sjosten snatched a 4-2 from Simmons and Boocock, the latter looking way below his best at the rear. In heat eight, King's Lynn icon Betts produced a typically courageous ride, belting round the outside of Holmqvist as they roared into lap two and going on to win. But with Ashby at the back the scores stayed level at 24-24.

Heat nine saw the Swedes introduce Jansson as a reserve replacement for Nygren to partner Michanek against Collins and Louis. The nineteen-year-old PC proved his mettle by making the start and withstanding relentless pressure from Michanek to take three points, but Jansson bettered a disappointing Louis for third to keep it all square.

In heat ten, England produced a trump card in the form of reserve Betts, stepping in for Ashby. He scooted from the tapes to lead all the way, taking the not-insignificant scalp of the previously unbeaten Persson. However, after getting into difficulty on lap one, Wilson could make little impression on Sjosten for third as the stalemate continued.

Heat eleven brought probably the best race of the night. Simmons was drafted in to partner fellow reserve Betts instead of Boocock to take on Lofqvist and Holmqvist. It was the English duo who jetted from the tapes, but Lofqvist grabbed a handful of throttle to storm round Simmons on the first turn. Simmons tried desperately to respond and Lofqvist only just about shook him off by lap three. The diminutive Poole Pirate then set his sights on Betts, with some wide sweeps round the bends putting him right on the Englishman's tail on the last lap. Betts tried to cover the expected outside move on the last turn, but the crafty Swede suddenly switched his intentions to the inside and nipped underneath to snatch a sensational on-the-line win and force yet another 3-3.

England looked vulnerable in heat twelve with the Swedish big guns Michanek and Persson facing up to Wilson and Collins. Although 'Mich' made the start, the home duo tucked in behind him to keep the scores level into the critical final heat. Once again, England team manager Len Silver turned to his reserves and brought the pair of them in for the below-par Boocock and Louis. Meanwhile, the Swedes called upon Lofqvist and Sjosten, both little over five feet tall, but giants in the speedway world. For the first time all evening, Lofqvist made the start. But Betts and Simmons quickly made second and third their own and rode a safe four laps to ensure the 39-39 draw. Which meant that, after 312 races, the winners of the *Daily Mirror* International Tournament came down to a run-off between two men. For Swedish manager Christer Bergstrom, Michanek was the obvious choice after a strong display that had seen him collect eleven points. For England boss Silver, the nomination was less straightforward. Betts and Simmons had both caught the eye, skipper Wilson had the experience, but it was Collins who was handed the role. He was the only man to have

The battling Terry Betts.

headed Michanek and, despite his tender years, was demonstrating the right temperament for the big occasion.

There was a huge roar as they approached the starting gate and, as the tapes rose, the noise increased yet further as Collins bolted from the start to lead. But Michanek looked the faster rider and tested the young Belle Vue Ace with some intimidating inside thrusts on the first lap. Entering the second lap, the Swede tried the outside line and generated enough speed to attempt to muscle under Collins going into the third turn. But as he did, the Englishman tried to block the move. The pair clashed and Collins was sent skidding across the track and into the fence. It was a classic 'Did he fall or was he pushed?' decision for referee Arthur Humphrey. To the official's great credit he did not hesitate and made an instinctive call as he saw it. Unfortunately for Sweden, it was the white light that was flicked on to indicate Michanek's disqualification. Debate raged after the incident, with the rival team managers defending their riders. Bergstrom was unequivocal in his thoughts, saying: 'That was the worst decision I have ever seen.' Silver meanwhile chose his words a little more carefully. He said: 'Michanek made his own gap, but then he hit Collins. That's boring and the referee had to exclude him. It's a pity it had to happen like this. A draw would have been a fair result on the night. But the England boys worked so hard that we deserved to win overall.'

As for the riders themselves, they both acknowledged that there was contact, but not surprisingly had different interpretations. Michanek said: 'What is one to do with speedway? It is getting to the stage where they have to hold out a flag to indicate that somebody is going to pass another rider.' In contrast Collins said: 'The decision was right. I couldn't retain control after Michanek came into me.' Of course, the discussions continued, but the referee's decision was final and England were awarded the winner's trophy for a tournament that had everything – world-class riders, brilliant racing and ample controversy.

After the final, a special match took place between Great Britain and the Rest of the World. Inevitably the match lacked the edge of the main event and, despite the inclusion of Australian and New Zealand riders in the GB septet, the Rest ran out comfortable winners 48-30. Michanek gained a measure of revenge over Collins by beating him in both their meetings. The rivalry was not to end there though, and developed into something of a prominent theme of the 1973 season. The pair returned to Wembley for the World Team Cup final in September, where Michanek was only beaten by Collins, whose maximum inspired another England victory.

One month later on club duty, Collins beat Michanek in another run-off after Belle Vue and Reading had finished level on aggregate after the Knock-Out Cup final second leg at Manchester's Hyde Road. The race was widely lauded as the greatest ever with the duo exchanging the lead an incredible sixteen times – an apt conclusion to a season in which the duo had contributed so much excitement.

15 July 1973: Wembley: England v. Sweden, Daily Mirror International Tournament Final

ENGLAND

		1	2	3	4	5	6	Total	BP
1	Ray Wilson (Capt.)	3	2	0	1*	–	–	6	1
2	Martin Ashby	1	1*	0	–	–	–	2	1
3	Eric Boocock	0	0	–	–	–	–	0	–
4	Peter Collins	1*	3	3	2	–	–	9	1
5	John Louis	2	0	0	–	–	–	2	–
6	Malcolm Simmons (Res.)	3	2	2	1*	2	–	10	1
7	Terry Betts (Res.)	1	3	3	2	1*	–	10	1

SWEDEN

		1	2	3	4	5	6	Total	BP
1	Christer Lofqvist	2	2	3	3	–	–	10	–
2	Hasse Holmqvist	0	1*	2	0	–	–	3	1
3	Anders Michanek	3	3	2	3	–	–	11	–
4	Soren Sjosten	0	1	1*	0	–	–	2	1
5	Bernt Persson	3	3	2	0	–	–	8	–
6	Olle Nygren (Res.) (Capt.)	0	0	–	–	–	–	0	–
7	Tommy Jansson (Res.)	2	1	1*	1*	–	–	5	2

England skipper Ray Wilson.

Heat 1: Wilson, Lofqvist, Ashby, Holmqvist, 69.8 secs
Heat 2: Simmons, Jansson, Betts, Nygren, 69.6 secs
Heat 3: Persson, Louis, Collins, Sjosten, 70.4 secs
Heat 4: Michanek, Simmons, Jansson, Boocock, 69.6 secs
Heat 5: Collins, Lofqvist, Holmqvist, Louis, 69.6 secs
Heat 6: Michanek, Wilson, Ashby, Nygren, 69.4 secs
Heat 7: Persson, Simmons, Sjosten, Boocock, 70.0 secs
Heat 8: Betts, Holmqvist, Jansson, Ashby, 71.2 secs
Heat 9: Collins, Michanek, Jansson, Louis, 70.8 secs
Heat 10: Betts, Persson, Sjosten, Wilson, 70.6 secs
Heat 11: Lofqvist, Betts, Simmons, Holmqvist, 70.8 secs
Heat 12: Michanek, Collins, Wilson, Persson, 70.2 secs
Heat 13: Lofqvist, Simmons, Betts, Sjosten, 70.0 secs
Run-off: Collins (F), Michanek (EX) (awarded)

26 June 1976, Wembley

1976 Intercontinental Final

Since 1995, the Speedway Grand Prix Series has firmly established itself as the sport's premier competition. Before then, the World Individual Championship was decided through a series of qualifying meetings leading towards a winner-takes-all one-off final. Of course, the big night itself was invariably a great occasion. But for the speedway purist, the real excitement often lay in the route towards the final as riders engaged in some truly cut-throat racing, desperate to stay in contention for the sport's greatest prize. And there were fewer meetings that inspired such hectic racing as the Intercontinental final. The meeting was first staged in 1976, replacing the old European final as the final step for riders from Britain, Scandinavia, Australasia and USA to qualify for the World Individual final.

It is probably fair to say that the mid-1970s marked the start of a long period in the sport in which the above regions were the dominant speedway forces, as opposed to riders from Eastern Europe. Consequently, the line-up at Intercontinental finals would often be stronger than the field for the World final itself. Certainly the first incarnation of the meeting backs up that theory.

At Wembley's Empire Stadium on 26 June 1976, sixteen riders, all of whom would be worthy of a World final berth, gathered to sort out which eight would progress to the championship climax in Katowice, Poland just ten weeks hence. Kiwi great Ivan Mauger, winner of four World crowns to this point in his illustrious career, defending world champion Ole Olsen of Denmark and 1974 champion Anders Michanek of Sweden were the headline acts. But in John Louis and Malcolm Simmons, who had recently bagged the World Pairs Championship, thrill-a-minute superstar Peter Collins and emerging Northern talents Chris Morton and Doug Wyer, English supporters were hopeful they would have plenty to shout about. Disappointingly, only 26,000 of them turned up for the occasion. But if the usual Wembley atmosphere was in any way compromised, it was more than made up for by some quite stupendous action.

Perhaps it was something to do with the 90°C temperature as Aussie duo Phil Crump and Billy Sanders quickly acclimatised, finishing first and second in front of a less comfortable Bernt Persson of Sweden and Dag Lovaas of Norway in heat one. Heat two brought together the Battle of Britain with Simmons, Louis, Morton and Wyer set to clash. From the start it was Wyer on the inside gate who caused absolute chaos. The twenty-eight-year-old Sheffield Tiger gave Simmons a clout, who in turn hit Morton, before elbowing Louis wide on the first corner. As they emerged down the back straight, Simmons led after a smart cut-back, followed by Wyer, Morton and 'Tiger' Louis. The nineteen-year-old Belle Vue Ace Morton was looking particularly lively though and he cut inside Wyer at the end of the third lap. Louis tried a similar move on the final lap, but Wyer was aware of him and shut him out.

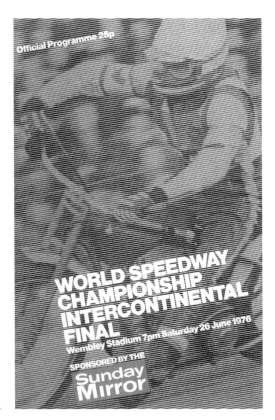

Programme cover.

Kiwi legend Ivan Mauger.

Heat three brought together Mauger and crowd favourite Collins for a mouthwatering head-to-head. But from the start it was underdogs John Boulger (Australia) and Scott Autrey (USA) who emerged in front. Mauger was in third and could make no inroads on the leading duo, particularly with Collins crawling all over his back wheel. Just for a moment it looked as though PC had sneaked round Mauger on the last-lap back straight but the typically ruthless Kiwi was having none of it and closed the gap to leave Collins pointless after one ride.

Heat four brought real controversy. In the first running, Olsen bent the tapes as they rose and Sjosten rode through them. German referee Gunther Sorber ruled an unsatisfactory start, with Olsen perhaps slightly fortunate not to be excluded for being the cause of the tapes being broken. His luck ended there though. In the second running, from gate four, Olsen made the break and on one wheel cut across the field, banging into Michanek en route to the inside line. Once again the red lights came on with Olsen's yellow exclusion light also being illuminated. The reason? Not maintaining a straight line until the thirty-yard marker. In the rerun, Sjosten showed briefly, but Michanek soon took over to bag an early win. So after one race each, pre-meeting favourites Olsen, Collins and Louis were all yet to get off the mark, while Mauger only had one.

Heat five pitched Olsen and Mauger in with the less fashionable Crump and Wyer. Olsen and Mauger were electric from the tapes with the former leading into the second lap. Suddenly though, the Dane spluttered to a halt with a seized engine. Mauger gratefully moved inside and Wyer round the outside for some gift points.

With no points after two rides, the world champion was now looking very vulnerable. Meanwhile, heats six and seven saw Englishmen Louis and Collins get their Championship campaigns back on track with fine wins. In the latter race, Simmons suffered misfortune by packing up while second to Collins. The next race really brought the crowd to their feet. Michanek led from the start with Boulger in hot pursuit, Morton was third after scorching round Persson on the first turn. Boulger continued to press the Swede continually on the outside and almost slipped by on the third lap. But on the final bend he was taken by surprise as young Morton, with arms and legs flailing everywhere, scampered by on the inside.

Next it was the turn of Morton's Belle Vue teammate Collins to serve up the thrills. Crump rode the twenty-two-year-old Englishman wide on the first turn and led down the back straight with Michanek and Louis challenging up the inside. A huge burst around the outside on the third and fourth turns saw Collins steam into second. With incredible control he then bravely rode within an inch of Crump's back wheel before swooping around him on the second turn of the second lap for a cracking win.

There was more English success in the following race as Wyer and his tassled leathers left the rest for dead as he cruised to victory. Morton returned to the fray in heat eleven, with the mighty Mauger among his opposition. It was the super-smooth Kiwi who galloped clear from the start with the youngster right on his tail. With the dirt moving to the outside, Morton took a huge handful of throttle at the

A difficult night for Danish legend and defending world champion Ole Olsen.

start of the second lap and roared around Mauger in spectacular style for a crowd-pleasing win.

Heat twelve was crunch-time for Olsen, now desperate for points if he was to have any chance of defending his World Championship crown in Katowice. But it was Simmons and Autrey who made the early running with Olsen in third. Machine difficulties for the American presented Olsen with an extra point, but at the interval stage he was sweating on just two points. Meanwhile, at the upper end of the scorechart, despite his inexperience at this level, Morton sat alongside Michanek with seven points in the lead.

Simmons virtually cemented his World final qualification by pocketing his third win of the evening in heat thirteen from Crump and Boulger. Heat fourteen put Olsen in with the two riders he probably would have least liked to face – Collins and Morton. The Belle Vue Aces had been the most dynamic riders on view, but Olsen simply had to get points against them. It was Morton who broke from the tapes, but on the first turn Collins was first to the dirt on the outside and stormed into the lead. Morton tried to get back on terms with his teammate on the next turn, but left a hole that Olsen duly exploited. The Dane set his sights on the lead, but with Morton proving to be something of a nuisance behind him, he could never really mount a challenge and had to settle for second. With just one ride left and a mere seven points the best that he could hope for, it was looking pretty bleak for Coventry's Danish star.

Heat fifteen saw Autrey take an impressive win to stand on the verge of being the first American world finalist in twenty-five years. Meanwhile, Wyer passed both Sanders and Michanek to continue his march towards Poland. Autrey's Exeter teammate Mauger won heat sixteen, with Louis taking a crucial second place. Crump took heat seventeen from Morton and Autrey to ensure all three of their World final places.

Interval leader Michanek streaked away from the tapes in heat eighteen, but with his form rapidly fading, he was overtaken first by Mauger and then Simmons to leave him far from safe on eight points. Results from the previous two heats had meant that it was now mathematically impossible for Olsen to finish in the top eight and he glumly finished second to Louis in heat nineteen, who in turn gave himself a chance of qualification with a gutsy win. Collins took the final programmed race – his fourth win in succession – from Wyer, whose consistent scoring had delivered him a richly deserved World final berth. But the fun was far from over and the final scorechart revealed that three run-offs would be required. Collins and Mauger had both gathered twelve points and would meet to decide the Intercontinental Champion, Crump and Simmons finished on eleven each and were to race for third and, most importantly of all, Louis and Michanek on eight points would race for the final qualification place.

Firstly it was Louis v. Michanek, with the crowd firmly on the side of the home man. Though the Ipswich skipper had been inconsistent, his Swedish rival had seen his touch desert him after winning his opening two rides. From the tapes it was a fairly level break, but Michanek used his inside starting position to push Louis wide on the first turn. The thirty-five-year-old Englishman kept his speed up though and used the drive out by the fence to lead down the back straight. The 1974 world champion chased hard for a couple of laps, but never looked like catching Louis, who was roared home by the patriotic supporters who could now celebrate all five English riders in the starting line-up making the cut for Poland.

Next up was Crump against Simmons, and it was the Newport-based Aussie who beat the Poole favourite to clinch third place. Finally, Mauger and Collins would meet to decide the winner of what had been an outstanding World Championship meeting. To cap just about the perfect day for English supporters, it was Collins who stormed to the victory over his illustrious rival. Mauger had lifted at the start and, despite some crafty inside thrusts, never looked like threatening Collins' lead.

It was a meeting that just about had it all: great racing, shocks, controversy and a popular home result. Of course, the main talking points were the quality of the Wembley track and the elimination of world champion Ole Olsen. On the racing surface, Mauger and Collins had high praise for Len Silver, who was charged with preparing the track for the occasion. In the week afterwards, the New Zealander commented: 'I have never known the Wembley track to be as good as it was on Saturday. It was a track on which riders could pass and at no time was it purely a matter of making the gate. I don't think I have ever seen as much passing in a big meeting and Len Silver deserves great credit from everyone in speedway.' Collins echoed the viewpoint, saying: 'The track was terrific and after all the trouble we had at the 1975 World final the riders as well as the spectators were relieved about that.'

Peter Collins went on to win the world championship that year.

But for Ole Olsen, the track was far from his thoughts. His lost world title was in the forefront of his mind and he held the referee Gunther Sorber personally responsible for his elimination. He said: 'There was nothing you could do about bad luck, which happened when the bike broke a piston in my second ride. But the referee was definitely wrong to exclude me in the previous race. Anders Michanek ran into me. I've got a bruise on my back to prove it. If he [the referee] thinks it was an unfair start then he should have stopped it and had all four back. I am very disappointed to be out of the World Championship, but then on the other hand I don't feel too bad, you can't race against the referee.'

Strong stuff. Naturally, it did not go without a response from the man with his finger on the button. Sorber said, 'I honestly believe that my decisions were right – for instance when Ole was excluded in heat four. I can understand how disappointed he must be after failing to qualify, but no referee can let personalities influence decisions. I know Ole, Ivan and Peter Collins and many of the riders from meetings in Germany. I know what it means for them to qualify for the World final. But the referee must always do what he believes to be right.'

Phil Crump won the run-off for third place.

26 June 1976, Wembley: Intercontinental Final

			1	2	3	4	5	Total
1	Phil Crump	Australia	3	1	2	2	3	11
2	Dag Lovaas	Norway	0	1	0	0	0	1
3	Billy Sanders	Australia	2	2	1	1	1	7
4	Bernt Persson	Sweden	1	0	0	1	1	3
5	Doug Wyer	England	1	2	3	2	2	10
6	John Louis	England	0	3	0	2	3	8
7	Malcolm Simmons	England	3	0	3	3	2	11
8	Chris Morton	England	2	2	3	1	2	10
9	Ivan Mauger	New Zealand	1	3	2	3	3	12
10	Scott Autrey	USA	2	2	1	3	1	9
11	Peter Collins	England	0	3	3	3	3	12
12	John Boulger	Australia	3	1	2	1	EX	7
13	Ole Olsen	Denmark	EX	RET.	2	2	2	6
14	Soren Sjosten	Sweden	1	0	RET.	N	N	1
15	Bengt Jansson	Sweden	2	1	1	EX	0	4
16	Anders Michanek	Sweden	3	3	1	0	1	8
17	Dave Jessup (Res.)	England	–	–	–	–	–	–
18	Phil Herne (Res.)	Australia	–	–	–	–	–	–
19	Soren Karlsson (Res.)	Sweden	–	–	–	–	–	–
TR	Trevor Geer	–		0	0	–	–	–
TR	Barry Thomas	–	–	–	–	–	–	–

Heat 1: Crump, Sanders, Persson, Lovaas, 68.4 secs

Heat 2: Simmons, Morton, Wyer, Louis, 69.0 secs

Heat 3: Boulger, Autrey, Mauger, Collins, 68.6 secs

Heat 4 (twice rerun): Michanek, Jansson, Sjosten, Olsen (EX), 69.4 secs

Heat 5: Mauger, Wyer, Crump, Olsen (RET.), 69.6 secs

Heat 6: Louis, Autrey, Lovaas, Sjosten, 69.2 secs

Heat 7: Collins, Sanders, Jansson, Simmons, 69.2 secs

Heat 8: Michanek, Morton, Boulger, Persson, 69.0 secs

Heat 9: Collins, Crump, Michanek, Louis, 68.8 secs

Heat 10: Wyer, Boulger, Jansson, Lovaas, 69.6 secs

Heat 11: Morton, Mauger, Sanders, Sjosten (RET.), 69.8 secs

Heat 12: Simmons, Olsen, Autrey, Persson, 69.0 secs

Heat 13: Simmons, Crump, Boulger, Greer, 70.0 secs

Heat 14: Collins, Olsen, Morton, Lovaas, 68.8 secs

Heat 15: Autrey, Wyer, Sanders, Michanek, 70.0 secs

Heat 16: Mauger, Louis, Persson, Jansson (EX), 69.4 secs

Heat 17: Crump, Morton, Autrey, Jansson, 69.8 secs

Heat 18: Mauger, Simmons, Michanek, Lovaas, 69.2 secs

Heat 19: Louis, Olsen, Sanders, Thomas, Boulger (EX), 68.8 secs

Heat 20: Collins, Wyer, Persson, Greer, 70.2 secs

Run-off for eighth place: Louis, Michanek, 68.6 secs

Run-off for third place: Crump, Simmons, 69.4 secs

Run-off for first place: Collins, Mauger, 68.2 secs

20 October 1979, Belle Vue

British League Riders Championship Final

Though these pages are packed with tales recounting classic speedway meetings, the sport is not always so thrilling. Most supporters have, at one time or other, sat through poor matches that were either one-sided or ruined by a badly prepared track. Sometimes there are fixtures where all the ingredients are in place for a feast of quality racing but, for one reason or another, the match never springs to life. Conversely, there are others that, on paper, look like run-of-the mill meetings but turn into thrill-a-minute spectacles. It is all part of the unpredictable nature of the sport.

But there was one meeting that fans from all over the UK could travel to with almost utter certainty that they were about to see something very special indeed, and that was the British League Riders Championship. The BLRC, as it was affectionately known, has been dressed up in many guises. Launched in 1965 with the formation of the British League, it was preceded by the Provincial League Riders Championship and has since been succeeded by the First Division and Elite League Riders Championships as the season's climax.

But most will agree that its glorious heyday came during the 1960s, 1970s and 1980s when the BLRC was the showpiece event of the British season and was staged at the spectacular Hyde Road circuit in Manchester, home of the Belle Vue Aces until its sad demise in 1987. Each of the sixteen riders in the line-up earned their place by topping their club's averages over the duration of each season. For many years, it was widely felt that the line-up was of an even higher quality than the World Individual Championship final itself. It all took place at a venue that invariably provided tremendous racing and, with the added attraction of the nearby zoological gardens and its funfair, it was a day out not to be missed for thousands of British speedway supporters.

Every year a packed crowd created a cracking Saturday night atmosphere and was rewarded with some truly exhilarating action. The 1979 staging was certainly no exception as 20,000 fans crammed into Hyde Road for a fantastic evening of drama and spectacle from the world's finest riders. New Zealand's Ivan Mauger, who had claimed his record-breaking sixth world title just a month earlier represented Hull, three-times world champion and four-times BLRC winner Ole Olsen was Coventry's contender and 1976 world champion and twice BLRC winner Peter Collins carried the home challenge for Belle Vue and England. The support cast wasn't too bad either, including explosive young English star Mike Lee of King's Lynn, American sensation Bruce Penhall of Cradley Heath and the super-smooth young Dane Hans Nielsen of Wolverhampton. With established international stars Scott Autrey (Exeter and USA), Malcolm Simmons (Poole and England), John Louis (Ipswich and England), Phil Crump (Swindon and England) and Gordon Kennett (Eastbourne and England) also in the line-up it was easy to see why the crowds had flocked to Manchester. Another

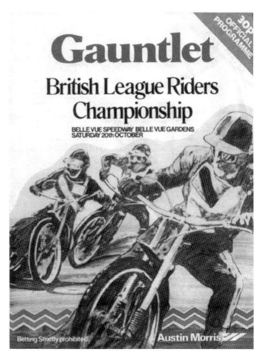

Programme cover.

King's Lynn's contender Michael Lee.

It was an uncharacteristically poor night for Ivan Mauger, seen here in Exeter colours.

interesting name in the line-up was Andy Grahame, who was representing Birmingham. The twenty-two-year-old had only ridden as the 'Brummies' stand-in at number eight all season, but had still managed to top their averages. With his full-time lower division club – Milton Keynes – he also finished as the top averaged rider. Consequently, he became the first and only rider ever to qualify for the British League and National League Riders Championships in the same season.

The opening heat saw the twenty-year-old Lee lay down a marker as he raced away from Nielsen, Kennett and Crump to win in a super-swift 69.2 seconds, a time that was to stand as the fastest of the evening. Simmons, New Zealander Larry Ross of Wimbledon and Penhall were the other winners in the first round of heats. Louis, Collins and Olsen each bagged a second place, while Mauger was among those who had only grabbed a third and was already facing an uphill struggle. Lee defeated the talented Californian Penhall in heat eight to be the only man unbeaten after two rides with six points. Meanwhile, wins for Louis and Collins put them alongside Penhall on five.

With an engine failure in heat six, Kiwi great Mauger had slipped out of contention with just one point from his opening outings. Penhall took heat nine to move up to eight points, after an opening race zero Crump took his second successive win in heat ten, while Collins missed out to Autrey in heat eleven.

Heat twelve was the final race before the interval and it brought Lee up against Olsen, Louis and Ross. After a thrilling tussle the thirty-eight-year-old 'Tiger' Louis delighted the Ipswich contingent with a fine victory, with Lee, Ross and Olsen finishing on his tail in that order.

At the interval stage, with every competitor having taken three rides, Lee, Louis and Penhall headed the leader board with eight points each. Collins was poised on seven and had still yet to meet the three leaders. Crump sat on six alongside Ross. Meanwhile Olsen and Mauger, now on four and three respectively, had already joined the ranks of the also-rans, though it was emerging that the latter was struggling with a back injury.

As the racing resumed in heat thirteen, it was the wily Louis who cranked up the pressure by moving into a clear lead with another victory. Crump continued his incredible revival as he won heat fourteen, Penhall responded by taking heat fifteen and there was a crucial result in heat sixteen. Collins won it, roared home by a passionate home support, but Lee could only finish third as the under-rated Aussie Titman split the Englishmen.

The meeting was building to a huge crescendo and all eyes were on the critical heat eighteen that pitted together Louis and Penhall, now both on eleven, Collins on ten and Crump on nine. All four could still conceivably win the title and as they approached the start gate there was a huge surge of cheers and horn blasts as the crowd readied themselves for around 70 seconds of spine-tingling speedway. As they streaked from the tapes, it was Penhall who made the break and looked set to win his first major title. Louis rode a tremendous first turn, gathering all the momentum he required to steam past on the back straight, but the American was not yet finished and over the ensuing four laps the duo swapped the lead a further five times with track expert Collins using every inch of the sweeping bends as he swarmed all over their back wheels.

In the end, however, it was Louis who prevailed, craftily sneaking inside Penhall on the final turn to win by half a length, with the ever-trying Collins in third. It gave Louis the title with fourteen points, Penhall finished second with thirteen while Lee's heat twenty victory gave him third with twelve. Louis was a popular and timely victor, coming, as it did, at the end of the veteran's testimonial season with his beloved Ipswich Witches. The Suffolk club had endured a tough year, finishing a lowly fifteenth in the British League and few could begrudge their battling skipper his crowning moment.

It is a meeting that Louis looks back on with a great deal of affection. 'At that time, the BLRC was such a tough meeting – harder than the World final, which always had a few of the Continental riders, who weren't really up to our level at that time. It was always a great atmosphere as well. The stadium was always packed out with supporters from all over the country. It was a fantastic track as well, it had so many racing lines – I had some great races with PC (Peter Collins) there. On this particular night, I was beaten by Malcolm Simmons in my first race and then I went through the card after that. It all boiled down to me and Bruce Penhall and we had a cracking race. We were swapping lines all the way and passed each other six times – it was one of the most enjoyable races I ever had. We took it in turns to try the inside and the outside. It was a long way round at the old Belle Vue but sometimes you could get that little bit of extra grip out wide. I remember Bruce going right out to the fence on the last turn to get some grip, so I chopped back really tight, used the slope, clipped the kerb and just managed to pip him by half a length. I was the oldest rider in the field and I don't think Bruce was too happy about being beaten by me! I didn't go to Belle Vue with massive hopes of winning. It was a meeting I was looking forward to, and wanted to do well in, but it was towards the end of the season and I was running out of stuff. I remember that night in the pits before the meeting. I had only taken one bike up to Belle Vue, whereas some of the other boys had three with them. I was also the only one to have Dunlop tyres on – everyone else had Pirellis on. I said to my mechanic John Bloomfield that perhaps we ought to switch, but he said: "You've used Dunlop all year and done okay, so why change now?" So I stuck with the Dunlop and it worked out okay for me. It's the type of small decision that doesn't seem to mean much at the time, but afterwards you look back and wonder if that made the difference. It was an absolutely great night. I must have tried everywhere to get film footage of that meeting, but cannot get any. The meeting was due to be televised by the BBC and cameras were there, but the meeting was never broadcast.'

His search for footage may never succeed but, like many fellow riders and supporters, the images of a packed Hyde Road on BLRC night are unlikely to ever leave him and will remain forever etched in the mind. Allan Morrey is one such person for whom the BLRC will always be a cherished memory. Morrey first began work at Belle Vue Speedway in 1944 before becoming Clerk of the Course in 1958, a role he only relinquished in 2004, at the end of the Aces seventeenth successive season at their replacement home at Kirkmanshulme Lane. He said: 'We had some big meetings at Hyde Road over the years, including the World Team Cup and World Pairs Finals, but the BLRC was always the highlight. Crowds came from all over Britain for the meeting – there were Exeter fans there all dressed in green and white and Edinburgh fans in blue and yellow – they came from everywhere, full of enthusiasm chanting for their riders. It was such a great track as well, with so many racing lines. As a host for the championships it was very neutral – it wasn't really any advantage for the home riders, who didn't really win it that often anyway. The winner was the best man on the night, simple as that. I remember when John Louis won it though. It was great for John

Cradley Heath's classy American Bruce Penhall.

Following pages: Peter Collins (left) and John Louis, two of the main contenders.

because he'd just missed out a few times in the 1970s and when he did win it, he wasn't one of the favourites at all.'

Despite the happy memories, Morrey has always been terribly saddened at the demise of the old Hyde Road Stadium, which was demolished in 1987 when owner Stuart Bamforth sold the land to a vehicle auctioning company. He says: 'Whenever I drive past the site, I have to look the other way. It still upsets me that it is gone.'

It is a comment that will resonate with anyone who witnessed the magical racing conjured up by the old track, particularly for those who were lucky enough to be in Manchester on BLRC night when the city's 'Theatre of Dreams' was speedway's Hyde Road rather than football's Old Trafford.

20 October 1979: Belle Vue: British League Riders Championship

			1	2	3	4	5	Total
1	Gordon Kennett	Eastbourne	1	0	0	0	0	1
2	Phil Crump	Swindon	0	3	3	3	0	9
3	Hans Nielsen	Wolverhampton	2	2	1	2	2	9
4	Mike Lee	King's Lynn	3	3	2	1	3	12
5	John Davis	Reading	0	1	2	0	1	4
6	Ivan Mauger	Hull	1	0	2	0	3	6
7	John Louis	Ipswich	2	3	3	3	3	14
8	Malcolm Simmons	Poole	3	0	0	1	1	5
9	Peter Collins	Belle Vue	2	3	2	3	1	11
10	Larry Ross	Wimbledon	3	2	1	1	3	10
11	Andy Grahame	Birmingham	0	0	1	0	0	1
12	Ian Cartwright	Halifax	1	1	1	2	0	5
13	Ole Olsen	Coventry	2	2	0	2	1	7
14	Scott Autrey	Exeter	1	1	3	1	2	8
15	John Titman	Leicester	0	1	0	2	2	5
16	Bruce Penhall	Cradley Heath	3	2	3	3	2	13

Heat 1: Lee, Nielsen, Kennett, Crump, 69.2 secs

Heat 2: Simmons, Louis, Mauger, Davis, 72.0 secs

Heat 3: Ross, Collins, Cartwright, Grahame, 70.8 secs

Heat 4: Penhall, Olsen, Autrey, Titman, 71.4 secs

Heat 5: Collins, Olsen, Davis, Kennett, 71.6 secs

Heat 6: Crump, Ross, Autrey, Mauger (ret.), 72.0 secs

Heat 7: Louis, Nielsen, Titman, Grahame, 71.8 secs

Heat 8: Lee, Penhall, Cartwright, Simmons, 71.6 secs

Heat 9: Penhall, Mauger, Grahame, Kennett, 72.0 secs

Heat 10: Crump, Davis, Cartwright, Titman, 72.0 secs

Heat 11: Autrey, Collins, Nielsen, Simmons, 71.8 secs

Heat 12: Louis, Lee, Ross, Olsen, 71.4 secs

Heat 13: Louis, Cartwright, Autrey, Kennett, 72.2 secs

Heat 14: Crump, Olsen, Simmons, Grahame, 73.4 secs

Heat 15: Penhall, Nielsen, Ross, Davis, 72.4 secs

Heat 16: Collins, Titman, Lee, Mauger, 72.6 secs

Heat 17: Ross, Titman, Simmons, Kennett, 72.0 secs

Heat 18: Louis, Penhall, Collins, Crump, 73.0 secs

Heat 19: Mauger, Nielsen, Olsen, Cartwright, 72.4 secs

Heat 20: Lee, Autrey, Davis, Grahame, 72.6 secs

9 August 1980

Halifax *v.* Hackney: British League

Though they were riding high at the top of the British League table in a season that had crossed the halfway stage, few were paying much credence to the championship challenge of Hackney Hawks in August 1980. After all, the East London team were the recipients of the wooden spoon in the preceding two seasons. This time round though, the emergence of classy Dane Bo Petersen as a genuine top-liner to go alongside dependable fellow countryman Finn Thomsen and spectacular Pole Zenon Plech had given them a genuine cutting edge at the top end of the team.

With Bristolian prospect Sean Willmott, improving Pole Roman Jankowski and seasoned professionals Barry Thomas and Keith White also in the line-up, the Hawks possessed a pretty solid 1-7. But was this really a septet capable of going the whole way? Surely they were far less equipped than Coventry, an awesome gathering of talent from home and abroad led by the truly great Dane Ole Olsen, winner of three World Individual Championships, and guided by the astute management of Peter Adams? The Bees had a 'been there, done that' arrogance about them – quite right too, as they had finished at the very opposite end of the table to Hackney in 1978 and 1979, taking back-to-back British League Championships. And what of Reading? Under the guidance of the flamboyant Dave Lanning, the Racers had invested heavily to put together a power packed line-up, including Swedish number one Jan Andersson, American sensation Bobby Schwartz, English Test star John Davis, Czech champion Jiri Stancl and Tony Briggs, son of all-time great New Zealander Barry. Yes, the Hawks had done well to last this far, but when they headed north to take on Halifax Dukes at their high-speed raceway The Shay for a British League fixture on Saturday 9 August 1980, there was real feeling that this was the place where they would be found out as to whether they were contenders or mere pretenders. With its strange grey shale, hugely banked bends and solid steel fence, the Yorkshire venue was a frightening prospect for many a visiting side and especially so for 'southern pansies', as many in the local crowd may have viewed the opposition.

If any team wanted to prove their character, Halifax was the place to do it. But in the opening heats it was the Hawks who were flapping as the Dukes ruled the roost, led by their cocky youngster Kenny Carter. Carter was only into his third year of racing, but was already an England international and was virtually unbeatable around The Shay. He won heat one in quite dismissive fashion from Hawks' number one Thomsen in a super-swift 63.3 seconds, a time that would stand as the night's fastest by more than two seconds.

The home side were operating the rider replacement facility for Norwegian Tormod Langli at number two, who, having ridden just one match for Halifax at the start of the season, broke his arm in a hang-gliding accident and never returned to

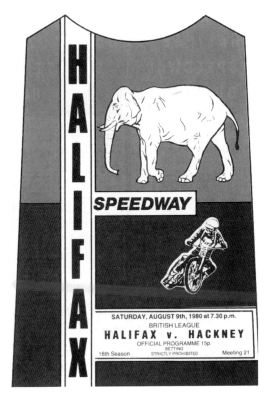

Programme cover.

action. Western Australian Merv Janke stepped in for heat one and finished ahead of Hawks' skipper Thomas to give the Dukes a 4-2. Heat two saw a Polish 1-2, Hackney's Jankowski leading home Halifax's Piotr Pyszny. With Craig Pendlebury in third and White at the rear, the Dukes maintained their two-point lead at 7-5.

Heat three saw another Pole enter the fray. Plech was the current world number two and one of the sport's most daring racers. Some of the other Hackney riders may have been easing themselves in gently, but Plech was never likely to take that route. He fought off the threats of Halifax's Aussie partnership of Janke and Mick McKeon to take the win. With Willmott at the rear, another 3-3 put the running scores at 10-8.

Heat four brought two of the meeting's top men together. Ian Cartwright was the Dukes' captain, a reliable scorer who had also represented his country and Petersen a dashing young Dane who was now averaging over ten points a match for the Hawks. However, it was Halifax's reserve Pyszny who exploited the first-bend banking to move into the lead. Tracked by Cartwright, the Dukes were set for a crucial 5-1. In his desperation to get back on terms, Petersen came to grief and, with White having tailed off with engine troubles, it was a 5-0 to Halifax. A seven-point lead was increased to nine by the completion of the next heat when McKeon and Janke scored a 4-2 over Thomsen and an out-of-touch Thomas.

A difficult situation was quickly developing into a crisis for the Championship-chasing Hawks as the Dukes slammed home another 5-1 in the following race. The

Above: Halifax skipper Ian Cartwright.

Right: Dependable Dane Finn Thomsen.

in-form Carter and Pyszny combined to defeat Petersen, possibly still shaken after his heat four spill, and Jankowski.

Plech took heat seven, but with Willmott a distant last behind Pyszny and Cartwright, the Hawks' cause was looking lost. In heat eight Thomsen was introduced as a tactical substitute instead of Thomas and Jankowski replaced fellow reserve White. But Halifax had the perfect counter punch with Carter stepping in to take his rider replacement ride. He cruised to his third win with Thomsen second, Pendlebury third and Jankowski at the back. With just five heats remaining, Halifax were fifteen points to the good and a real thrashing for the Hawks was on the cards.

Heat nine marked a revival for the Hawks with Petersen and Jankowski producing a beautiful team ride to see off McKeon and Janke for a 5-1. Team manager Dave Erskine's faith in Jankowski was crucial. The Pole had recorded last places in his previous two outings and he may have been forgiven for opting for Plech for a tactical outing. His decision to keep this particular ace in hand was to prove pivotal.

Still eleven points in arrears, heat ten saw Petersen brought in to replace Willmott to partner the previously unbeaten Plech. It was a heat that brought together the big guns, with Halifax skipper Cartwright taking his rider replacement outing to partner Carter, who was also unbeaten. At the first turn it was the Hawks who emerged in front with Carter having missed the gate completely. Unfortunately for Halifax,

Hawks' Bo Petersen (centre), seen here with fellow Danes Jens Rasmussen (left) and Finn Thomsen.

Cartwright was unable to breach the blocking tactics of Plech and Petersen as they scored a second successive 5-1 for Hackney.

At 33-26, the Hawks were still more than six points behind and could therefore introduce Plech as a tactical substitute in heat eleven. The Hawks gathered yet further momentum as Thomsen and Plech slammed in a third successive maximum heat win from Cartwright and Pendlebury.

Heat twelve reunited Plech and Petersen against Carter and McKeon. Plech was sitting on a paid maximum, but Carter was hell bent on not letting him have it as he roared out of the start. Unfortunately for him his machine was not up to it and he ground to a halt with a seized engine. Plech completed an impressive maximum and, with Petersen easily holding off McKeon, it was a fourth 5-1 on the bounce for Hackney. Incredibly, from being on the verge of an embarrassing defeat, the Hawks were now in front at 35-36. But with no Petersen or Plech in the last heat, victory was still far from certain.

The Dukes pitched the impressive reserve Pyszny in instead of Janke to partner skipper Cartwright. For the Hawks the solid Thomsen was to be paired with Jankowski, another reserve replacement, stepping in for Willmott, who had been badly off the pace. Hackney needed to share the spoils for a narrow win with Halifax looking for a 4-2 or better to save their blushes. A thrilling battle ensued with the Hawks duo making the early running. But a determined ride from Pyszny took him past both

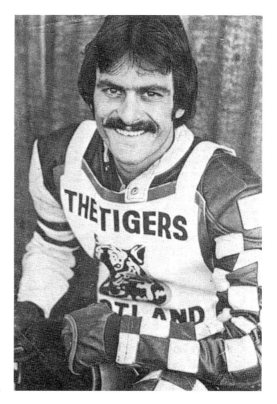

Dukes' Aussie star Mick McKeon.

Hackney's spectacular Zenon Plech.

Jankowski and then Thomsen to lead. The speedy Pole never looked like being caught and with Thomsen safely tucked in second it was the vital third place that the whole match now hinged on. Jankowski and Cartwright passed and repassed with the Hawks reserve eventually just hanging on for the critical point.

The 39–38 victory was – and still is – one of the most amazing comebacks in British speedway history. From a seemingly hopeless position of fifteen points behind after eight races, the Hawks rallied to win the last five races 23-7. What is even more remarkable is that they did it with three riders not contributing any points. Barry Thomas, Keith White and Sean Willmott all failed to score. But the never-say-die attitudes of Plech, Thomsen, Petersen and Jankowski, coupled with some fine tactical moves by Dave Erskine, made this match one of the most fondly thought of in the Hawks' history.

Paul Tadman was one such Hackney fan who enjoyed the spectacle in person. On the night he was perched with the rest of the Hawks supporters on the fourth bend terracing. 'Things like that just did not happen, especially with Hackney's reputation at Halifax,' he recalls. 'No-one could quite believe it – even the riders looked shocked when they came round afterwards on the victory parade. After heat eight, we all started joking among ourselves, "right, just four 5-1s now", then it became three, then two then one. It really was incredible.'

He also paid tribute to maximum man Plech, a cult hero in Hackney Speedway circles. 'Zenon could ride absolutely any track, big, small, whatever. It just depended on whether he clicked on the night or not. On that particular night, he was brilliant, he even won the second-half final as well.'

On the subject of Plech, there was a lovely observation from 'Hawkeye', the irreverent contributor to the Hackney matchday programme, in the following week's issue. He wrote: 'Zenon was the star of the night here and had a most fruitful evening, scoring fourteen plus one bonus. The *Sunday Mirror* endorsed this viewpoint by naming him as Z. Peach in their results column.'

Hackney's Len Silver was not present at The Shay on the famous night, but wrote the following in the same programme: 'My mind is in a state of hazy excitement as I write these notes late on Saturday evening having just received the news that Dave Erskine, my fellow team manager, has masterminded the most fantastic victory any team is ever likely to enjoy and in so doing has placed the magnificent seven into a position where the league championship is really within our grasp.' He goes on to describe the feat in the following glowing terms: 'The fight back must go down in British League history as the most outstanding ever.'

Indeed, the meeting has probably stood the test of time as just about the greatest – and unlikeliest – of all comebacks, particularly with The Shay being such a difficult place for away riders to adapt to. Dukes' skipper on the night, Ian Cartwright, looks back on the now-defunct track with great affection, but also reveals that it was an intimidating prospect for some opponents. He said: 'Some people would turn up for the first time, take one look over the fence and say "blimey – how on earth are we going to get round this place!" They would be beaten even before the first race.'

Not so the Hawks, and the victory really did set them for a genuine title tilt. Sadly though, their championship dream did not come true. They were eventually pipped by Reading, who took the 1980 British League with 49 points, with Hackney second on 46, Belle Vue third on 43 and Coventry fading to fourth with 42. But it was a fine season where they proved themselves as a real force to be reckoned with and, for one particular summer's night in Yorkshire, anything seemed possible for Hackney Hawks.

9 August 1980: Halifax *v.* Hackney: British League

HALIFAX		1	2	3	4	5	6	Total	BP
1	Kenny Carter	3	3	3	0	EF	–	9	–
2	Tormod Langli R/R	–	–	–	–	–	–	–	–
3	Ian Cartwright (Capt.)	2*	1*	1	1	0	–	5	2
4	Mick McKeon	1*	3	1	1	–	–	6	1
5	Merv Janke	1	2	1	0	–	–	4	–
6	Piotr Pyszny (Res.)	2	3	2*	2	3	–	12	1
7	Craig Pendlebury (Res.)	1*	1	0	–	–	–	2	1

HACKNEY		1	2	3	4	5	6	Total	BP
1	Finn Thomsen	2	2	2	3	2	–	11	–
2	Barry Thomas (Capt.)	0	0	–	–	–	–	0	–
3	Bo Petersen	F	1	3	2*	2*	–	8	2
4	Sean Willmott	0	0	–	–	–	–	0	–
5	Zenon Plech	3	3	3	2*	3	–	14	1
6	Roman Jankowski (Res.)	3	0	0	2*	1*	–	6	2
7	Keith White (Res.)	0	EF	–	–	–	–	0	–

Heat 1: Carter, Thomsen, Janke, Thomas, 63.3
Heat 2: Jankowski, Pyszny, Pendlebury, White, 65.6 secs
Heat 3: Plech, Janke, McKeon, Willmott, 65.9 secs
Heat 4: Pyszny, Cartwright, Petersen (F), White (EF), 54.4 secs
Heat 5: McKeon, Thomsen, Janke, Thomas, 65.7 secs
Heat 6: Carter, Pyszny, Petersen, Jankowski, 65.7 secs
Heat 7: Plech, Pyszny, Cartwright, Willmott, 66.1 secs
Heat 8: Carter, Thomsen, Pendlebury, Jankowski, 65.5 secs
Heat 9: Petersen, Jankowski, McKeon, Janke, 66.6 secs
Heat 10: Plech, Petersen, Cartwright, Carter, 65.8 secs
Heat 11: Thomsen, Plech, Cartwright, Pendlebury, 67.9 secs
Heat 12: Plech, Petersen, McKeon, Carter (EF), 66.6 secs
Heat 13: Pyszny, Thomsen, Jankowski, Cartwright, 67.1 secs

5 September 1981, Wembley

World Championship Final

A book of this type would not be complete without the inclusion of the 1981 World Individual Championship final. It is a meeting that is held up as one of the sport's greatest occasions and the one that all other classic speedway meetings are invariably measured against. Whenever and wherever speedway supporters gather to discuss the 'greatest meeting ever' the case for the '81 final' is inevitably aired. As a consequence, its reputation seems to grow year on year.

It all took place at Wembley's Empire Stadium, the spiritual home of the World final, on 5 September, in front of a packed crowd of 92,000, where an all-star cast of riders vied for the sport's biggest prize of all. England's Michael Lee was defending the title he had won the previous year in Gothenburg, Sweden. But it had been a difficult preceding twelve months for the wayward twenty-two-year-old. He had suffered the wrath of the authorities for his unexplained absence from several important fixtures during the season and, even more controversially, had picked up a criminal record for the possession of cannabis. He had not been the role model the sport had hoped for and it was a distinctly muted reception that greeted his introduction in the stadium as the reigning world champion.

Also in the line-up was the man who many saw as the champion-in-waiting, the charismatic and spectacular American sensation Bruce Penhall. The previous year the twenty-four-year-old had departed Gothenburg heart-broken as he saw his title challenge come to nothing. But, after a superb 1981, which had seen him win the World Pairs Championship with Bobby Schwartz in Poland, triumph at the Intercontinental final in Denmark and lead the British League averages with an incredible eleven-point-plus match average for Cradley Heath, he arrived at Wembley as the bookmakers' clear favourite to win the title.

In his way stood some formidable opposition, led by the legendary Dane Ole Olsen, winner of three World Individual Championships and more pertinently, the previous two Wembley finals. Though now thirty-four, anyone who underestimated Olsen did so at their peril. He was a man who had proved time and time again that he could rise to the occasion. Then there were the rest of the English challengers, Kenny Carter, Dave Jessup and Chris Morton, all well capable of beating the world's best on their day. Although he was in his first final, twenty-year-old Carter insisted that he was not just in it for the experience and told anyone who would listen: 'I'm going there to win it.'

Young Danes Hans Nielsen, Erik Gundersen and Tommy Knudsen were relatively new to this level; indeed, for the latter two, the evening marked their World final debuts but all three had been among the best riders in Britain all year and looked ripe for the big-time. Sweden's Jan Andersson had finished fourth in 1980 and was still

Programme cover.

Erik Gundersen was
super-fast.

improving, while the likes of New Zealand's Larry Ross, Germany's Egon Muller and
Poland's Zenon Plech had carved out fine reputations on the international stage and
were nobody's mugs. It had all the ingredients of a classic final and, with a seemingly
immaculate racing strip prepared by Hackney promoter Len Silver, the crowd braced
themselves for a thrilling evening.

Heat one pitted Olsen against fellow countryman and Coventry teammate Knudsen,
Ross and experienced Pole Edward Jancarz. In a close start it was Olsen who emerged
first from gate three but, hugging the white line, Knudsen cut inside his more illustrious
colleague and roared away to take three points in his first-ever World final ride.

Heat two brought Englishmen Carter and Morton together with experienced
continentals Muller and Plech. Rather surprisingly it was the latter who was first to

show, leading for the first half-lap. But on the third turn, Carter drove underneath him and by the next bend Morton had gone by. A flustered Plech slid off as Carter held on for a fine win. Though it was early days yet, heat three had all the makings of being a crunch race, bringing together four genuine title hopes in Lee, Penhall, Gundersen and Andersson. Crucially, the American made the jump and led into the first turn. Lee tried the big sweep around the boards but was shut out by Gundersen and Andersson. Looking speedy, the Dane chased his Cradley Heath teammate, but Penhall held on for an important win. Lee finished last, his hopes of retaining his crown all but gone.

Heat four saw Jessup utilising his super-fast gating ability to scorch away from Nielsen and Czechoslovakian rank outsiders Jiri Stancl and Ales Dryml for three points. The next race saw Carter make a mess of the start and, though he was quickly past Dryml and Jancarz, Lee was a different proposition and he was forced to settle for second behind the defending champion.

Heat six matched young Danes Gundersen and Knudsen together with Plech and Stancl. It was a hard-fought first turn, but Gundersen used the grip around the outside to scoot clear. After an immaculate four laps, it was hardly surprising when it was announced that the track record had fallen to the twenty-one-year-old with a searing 66.8 seconds.

Heat seven pitched pre-meeting favourites Penhall and Olsen in with potential spoilers Nielsen and Muller. On paper it looked like the makings of a good race, but on shale it was pure dynamite. Olsen burst from gate four to lead into the first turn from Nielsen. But Penhall was swiftly into action and shoved Nielsen aside to take second as they headed down the back straight. Riding with beautiful fluency, Olsen maintained his lead with Penhall riding right on the limit in an attempt to reel him in and, by the third lap, the American had moved right up onto the Dane's back wheel. He attempted to sweep around him on turns three and four, but the crafty thirty-four-year-old covered the move. Even when Penhall tried to sneak inside on the home straight, he found his path blocked by Olsen, who was riding as if he had eyes in the back of his crash helmet. The race was reaching boiling point and the pair swung into turns one and two of the final lap at high speed, struggling to maintain control. Indeed, they both lifted simultaneously and almost identically as they exited the second turn. At first it looked as if Penhall was going to attempt to muscle under Olsen going into the last bend, but instead he chose the big drive round the boards. Momentarily, it seemed as if he had gone far too wide, with Olsen taking the short route on the white line. But the American generated tremendous speed out wide and, as he brought his wheels into line, he began to eat into Olsen's lead on the run-in to the finish. The crowd were at fever pitch as the pair flashed across the line together, with Penhall just having sneaked past to win by half-a-wheel for an incredible win. It was one of the great World final rides, a from-the-back ride to beat one of the sport's all-time greats right on the line. Fantastic stuff!

The crowd were just about getting their breath back when the riders began to line up for heat eight. At the first attempt Ross broke the tapes and Polish reserve Henryk

Tommy Knudsen, Danish
sensation.

Olszak stepped into the breach, but he could make little impact in a processional race won by Jessup from Andersson and Morton. Jessup now joined Penhall as the only men unbeaten after two rides each. Intriguingly, the pair were due to clash in the next race, with Jancarz and Plech destined for bit-part roles. Jessup was on gate two, but it was Penhall from four who made it to the first turn ahead. Well aware of the Englishman's threat, he expertly swung across the field and blocked any possible inside challenge. With the crowd getting behind him, Jessup put everything into the chase and almost nipped inside the American on the third lap, but by the final bend he was beaten. Suddenly and heart-breakingly, Jessup's machine spluttered to a halt as he exited the last turn, leaving the two Poles to pick up the minor places and his Wembley dreams once again in tatters due to engine failure, much as they had been in 1978 at the same venue.

Heat ten saw young guns Carter and Knudsen, both with a healthy five points under their belts at that stage, back in action. Swede Andersson showed briefly but Carter and Knudsen flashed past on either side down the back straight. Knudsen provided a brief threat to Carter's lead but, by the final lap, the cocky youngster was waving to the crowd as he claimed his second win.

Heat eleven brought together previous champions Lee and Olsen. By now he was all too aware of the extra drive on the outside and Olsen used it to go clear on the back straight to win from Lee and Morton. Heat twelve saw another contender fall by the wayside. Gundersen's bike had carried him to the track record in his previous outing, but it let him down this time as he stopped while leading on the second lap as Muller took a lucky win. At the interval stage, Penhall sat at the top of the pile with nine points, followed by Carter on eight, with the duo still set to meet in heat twenty. Meanwhile, Olsen and Knudsen were poised on seven each.

As far as the title picture was concerned, heat thirteen was irrelevant, but Andersson gave the Swedish fans something to cheer as he won from Muller, Jancarz and Stancl. Heat fourteen saw the reappearance of Penhall. This time he had Knudsen as his main threat and if anyone in the stadium thought they could not possibly see another race like heat seven, they were about to be proved drastically wrong. As they surged from the tapes, Knudsen on gate one and Penhall on gate four immediately went looking for each other, with Morton and Dryml reluctant spectators. Knudsen drove straight to the outside in an apparent attempt to counter any outside blast from Penhall. But the American had read his mind and brilliantly cut back underneath him to take the lead. Then, in an incredible move, Knudsen came from nowhere to scream back inside Penhall on the back straight, much to the delight of the crowd who roared their approval. For two laps the young Dane looked to have the measure of the American but, by the end of lap three, Penhall had made serious inroads and was preparing to mount his challenge. Grabbing a handful of throttle he blasted around the outside on the first bend of the final lap to draw level and, with the crowd going crazy, the pair raced neck and neck down the back straight. Both riders dived into the final turn racing right on the limit, with Penhall out wide and Knudsen mid-track. As they headed towards the finish, it became a virtual drag race to the line and though Knudsen held a narrow advantage, Penhall was reeling him in inch-by-inch. The pair crossed the line together, almost impossible to separate. Both riders punched the air at the race's conclusion, convinced they had won, as the crowd awaited the verdict from the referee's box. The announcer revealed that the American had just got the verdict, a judgement later confirmed by TV coverage who had Penhall ahead by no more than the width of a tyre. He had done it again! One on-the-line win was amazing enough, but two was simply unbelievable. Once the crowd had regathered their senses, they were faced with another dramatic twist in the plot. Carter, Jessup, Olsen and Gundersen emerged for heat fifteen with the former looking like the only realistic threat to Penhall at that stage. For the third time that night, it was Jessup who made the trap and led down the back straight from Carter, Gundersen and Olsen. The younger Dane then swept around Carter on the third and fourth turn to relegate the Englishman to third. But on entering the second lap, Carter's title hopes vanished completely when his machine died on him. Quite amazingly, the same fate awaited Jessup and he packed up on the last lap while leading to compound an already rotten run of luck. Gundersen won with a fortunate Olsen taking second.

Heat sixteen saw a surprise winner in the form of Ross, with Lee relegated to last, by now well resigned to the loss of his crown. With one ride left for all riders, Penhall

Kenny Carter, one of England's hopes.

was three points clear of the chasing pack on a maximum twelve as all eyes turned to heat twenty, where he could clinch the crown.

Heat seventeen saw Gundersen win from Nielsen to finish on eleven points for a fine World final debut. Knudsen won the next to go to twelve and guarantee himself a spot on the rostrum and Olsen joined his young teammate on the same score by romping away with heat nineteen. But the moment the crowd and indeed Penhall himself had been waiting for arrived. He coasted to the tapes for heat twenty, needing just a single point from a race that included Ross, Carter and Stancl to be absolutely certain of the title. The tapes rose and Carter and Penhall hit the first turn together but, rather than engage in combat, the American seemed content to let the Halifax man go clear and settle for second. As they entered the final lap, Penhall took a big look over his shoulder to check on the whereabouts of Ross and Stancl, but they were well in arrears. He then rode a conservative final lap but, as he exited the final turn, he pulled an enormous wheelie to celebrate the sweetest moment of his career.

As he returned to the pits he was engulfed by fans, well-wishers, Cradley Heath colleagues, manager Peter Adams and teammate Erik Gundersen and his family from America. The deposed champion Michael Lee leant over the throng and congratulated the new number one, saying: 'Well done Bruce – the best man tonight by far.' A sentiment few would have disagreed with.

Olsen beat Knudsen in a run-off for second, but by then the party was well underway as an emotional Penhall dedicated his victory to his parents, who had both been tragically killed when their private plane crashed in 1975. He said: 'My mother never watched me race speedway but my dad said that as long as I enjoyed the sport I could carry on and he would give me all the help I wanted so I really wanted to win the world championship for them… and for my brothers and sisters and everyone else who has helped and supported me. I came to the meeting very relaxed this year but the final race was a bit tense. I had one worry because I had to change my bike for that one. Pete Adams found traces of metal in the oil of my best bike and it could have seized up. So I went out on my number two bike just in case. Pete was terrific, he told me: "Take it easy and don't do anything stupid." I guess I looked behind a few times but I made it. I had hoped to make five starts, but it didn't work out that way and I had some really hard races. The race with Ole was really tight and the one with Tommy Knudsen even closer.'

It was an incredible evening for speedway, a packed crowd witnessing superb racing and the coronation of a great champion. Looking back then, it seems quite ironic that, rather than marking the beginning of a golden era in the sport's history, it proved quite the opposite. Twelve months later, Penhall, the sport's figurehead and most recognisable figure, suddenly walked away from the sport. After claiming his second successive world title at the Los Angeles Coliseum, despite a controversial clash with Kenny Carter, he announced his retirement to pursue an acting career up the road at Hollywood.

Within a few short years, Carter and Australian superstar Billy Sanders were also lost to the sport when they died in separate tragic off-track circumstances. Speedway then lost another icon in Michael Lee, whose ongoing problems with the sport's authorities finally led to a long-term ban. Around the same time, in the mid-1980s, it was also announced that Wembley had closed its doors to speedway racing for good, making the 1981 World final the last meeting ever to take place within the famous venue.

Since the turn of the century, the advent of the Grand Prix Series has brought the sport back into the world's great stadiums and re-established its reputation internationally. But for many years following the 1981 World final many believed, and indeed some still do, that speedway racing could never be as good again.

5 September 1981: Wembley: World Championship Final

			1	2	3	4	5	Total
1	Edward Jancarz	Poland	1	1	1	1	1	5
2	Tommy Knudsen	Denmark	3	2	2	2	3	12
3	Ole Olsen	Denmark	2	2	3	2	3	12

Penhall chases Olsen in their classic encounter.

4	Larry Ross	New Zealand	0	EX	1	3	0	4
5	Kenny Carter	England	3	2	3	EF	3	11
6	Zenon Plech	Poland	F	0	2	1	0	3
7	Egon Muller	West Germany	1	1	3	2	2	9
8	Chris Morton	England	2	1	1	1	0	5
9	Michael Lee	England	0	3	2	0	F	5
10	Erik Gundersen	Denmark	2	3	0	3	3	11
11	Bruce Penhall	USA	3	3	3	3	2	14
12	Jan Andersson	Sweden	1	2	1	3	2	9
13	Ales Dryml	Czechoslovakia	0	0	2	0	1	3
14	Jiri Stancl	Czechoslovakia	1	1	0	0	1	3
15	Hans Nielsen	Denmark	2	0	0	2	2	6
16	Dave Jessup	England	3	3	EF	EF	1	7
17	Henryk Olszak (Res.)	Poland	0	–	–	–	–	–
18	Preben Eriksen (Res.)	Denmark	–	–	–	–	–	–

Heat 1: Knudsen, Olsen, Jancarz, Ross, 67.6 secs

Heat 2: Carter, Morton, Muller, Plech (F), 67.2 secs

Heat 3: Penhall, Gundersen, Andersson, Lee, 67.1 secs

Heat 4: Jessup, Nielsen, Stancl, Dryml, 68.1 secs

Heat 5: Lee, Carter, Jancarz, Dryml, 67.5 secs

Heat 6: Gundersen, Knudsen, Stancl, Plech, 66.8 secs

Heat 7: Penhall, Olsen, Muller, Nielsen, 68.1 secs

Heat 8 (rerun): Jessup, Andersson, Morton, Olszak (Ross, EX), 67.4 secs

Heat 9: Penhall, Plech, Jancarz, Jessup (EF), 67.4 secs

Heat 10: Carter, Knudsen, Andersson, Nielsen, 68.0 secs

Heat 11: Olsen, Lee, Morton, Stancl, 67.8 secs

Heat 12: Muller, Dryml, Ross, Gundersen, 68.2 secs

Heat 13: Andersson, Muller, Jancarz, Stancl, 67.6 secs

Heat 14: Penhall, Knudsen, Morton, Dryml, 68.0 secs

Heat 15: Gundersen, Olsen, Jessup (EF), Carter (EF), 67.9 secs

Heat 16: Ross, Nielsen, Plech, Lee, 68.1 secs

Heat 17: Gundersen, Nielsen, Jancarz, Morton, 67.6 secs

Heat 18: Knudsen, Muller, Jessup, Lee (F), 68.9 secs

Heat 19: Olsen, Andersson, Dryml, Plech, 68.3 secs

Heat 20: Carter, Penhall, Stancl, Ross, 67.6 secs

Run-off for second place: Olsen, Knudsen, 67.9 secs

14 August 1983

Mildenhall *v.* Newcastle: National League

During the late 1970s and early 1980s Newcastle and Mildenhall were two of the most dominant clubs in the National League, Britain's second tier of team speedway. Indeed, from 1976 until 1984, the two sides accumulated four National League Championships, were runners-up on five other occasions, won two National League Knock-Out Cup titles and four National League Four-Team Tournament Championships between them.

1982 was a particularly dominant season for Newcastle. A mighty Diamonds septet, consisting of National League giants Joe and Tom Owen, experienced Scotsman Bobby Beaton, swift Aussie Rod Hunter, solid second strings Alan Emerson and Keith Bloxsome and young reserve Rob Foy, simply bulldozed the opposition aside. They rode off with the National League Championship, National League KO Cup and National League Fours. For good measure, their kingpin Joe Owen also won the National League Riders Championship.

Mildenhall were the team that had pushed them hardest, finishing as runners-up in both the league and in the fours. In the league fixtures, the Fen Tigers took the points in the home match at West Row after a thrilling fixture had ended 49–47. But there was controversy in the Newcastle-hosted fixture when co-promoter Ian Thomas outwitted the East Anglians. The crafty Thomas had ordered tons of fresh shale to be spread over the Brough Park surface before the meeting, leaving a track that their visitors were quite unprepared for. By the time they had adjusted to the conditions it was too late as Newcastle whipped their chief rivals 61–35. The result and the manner of it left Mildenhall promoter Bernie Klatt blazing. 'I've never seen so much dirt on a track. Even the Newcastle riders were complaining,' he said. 'I think the Newcastle promoters, who are seen as notable personalities in the sport, must have felt embarrassed about their heap of a track because they didn't say a word to me after the match. The track was bad for both teams, but Newcastle's home knowledge got them through. Once we adapted to such unusual conditions we outscored them 25–23 in the last eight races. Given a decent track we would have pushed them very close.'

And thus an already intense rivalry was cranked up a notch or two. Following their blockbusting season, Newcastle were forced by the 45-point maximum average rule to weaken ahead of the 1983 season, giving Mildenhall an even greater opportunity of plugging the gap between the two sides. Newcastle shed Tom Owen and Bloxsome, leaving a top-heavy foursome of Joe Owen, Hunter, Beaton and Emerson to be supported by a regularly rotated group of inexperienced juniors. In contrast, Mildenhall went for a more solid line-up. Dependable skipper Robert Henry was to lead a side that also featured established scorers Derek Harrison, Richard Knight and Carl Baldwin, the promising Carl Blackbird and a new name on the scene, youngster

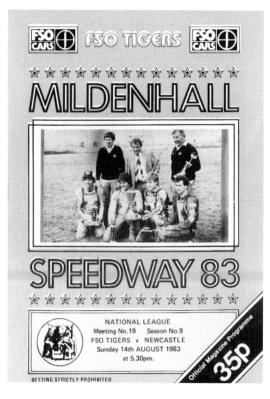

Programme cover.

Fen Tigers' captain Robert Henry.

David Jackson, who had been given a glowing reference by fellow countryman, the Aussie number one Billy Sanders.

The first league meeting between the two contenders took place at Brough Park on 25 July and was a real cracker. The home team won it 49-46 after a highly controversial final-race 5-0 for the Diamonds with both Fen Tigers Baldwin and Knight being excluded after clashes with Owen and Hunter.

So, when the teams reunited at West Row on 14 August for the return fixture the anticipation was huge. Both sides were, as expected, vying for the league championship and Mildenhall were thirsting for revenge. With just eleven matches remaining in the 1983 season, Newcastle led the table on 36 points, with the Fen Tigers second, poised on 30. It was a must-win match for the latter. They had to cut the gap to a workable four, and if it was to drift to eight then the league would be all but lost.

The home side tracked a familiar 1-7. Knight, Blackbird, Harrison, Baldwin and Henry formed the main body of the team with Jackson and local junior Ian Farnham at reserve. Meanwhile, Owen and Hunter led the visitors, but fellow heat-leader Beaton was absent due to leg and back injuries sustained at the fours finals at Peterborough. The rider replacement facility would cover for the heavy-scoring Scot. Alan Emerson was also suffering with a minor leg injury but still took his place in the pits. Martin Scarisbrick, Neil Barnsley and Lawrie Bloomfield completed the opposition line-up.

Fast Aussie Rod Hunter.

Scarisbrick, a Belle Vue asset, had emerged from the junior ranks to win a permanent slot in the side, even producing a title-winning performance in covering for Beaton at the fours finals as they pipped Mildenhall (who else?) to the crown. Australian Barnsley was also a regular but, holding an average of only around two points a match, he was an obvious weak link. Bloomfield, in contrast, was making his Diamonds debut on loan from Ipswich. A regular in the East Anglian Junior League and, crucially, someone with plenty of experience of the West Row circuit, he was a typically shrewd signing by Thomas.

On a lovely sunny Sunday evening, a 4,000 crowd crammed into the West Row expecting some ferocious speedway. But by 5.30 p.m. the wait was over as Knight, Blackbird, Hunter and Scarisbrick lined up for heat one. Around the first turn, Knight and Hunter were locked together but the Englishman held the better line down the straight and pulled clear. At the rear, Scarisbrick and Blackbird enjoyed a good scrap, with the former just managing to resist the latter's outside swoops for a 3-3.

Heat two brought the first real controversy of the evening. Barnsley made the gate from the inside, but outside him Farnham, Jackson and Bloomfield tangled in what looked like a clear case of first-bend bunching. But Jackson's red light was switched on and the Aussie was disqualified. In the rerun, Barnsley was the next to bite the dust, spinning over on the first turn. However, much to the consternation of the crowd, he was given the benefit of the doubt and allowed back into another restart. This time it was Bloomfield who made the gate and he streaked away in impressive style, no doubt raising a smile on the face of team manager Thomas. Farnham took second with Barnsley tailing off at the back.

Heat three brought Hunter back into the fray, to partner Emerson in a rider replacement ride against Baldwin and Henry. The Diamonds showed first but the bustling Baldwin burst past Emerson on the back straight and mounted a determined challenge over the ensuing laps, with Hunter just managing to stave him off. Henry, meanwhile, muscled his way inside Emerson on the penultimate lap to take third.

The next race saw the league's top rider Owen being introduced to the action and he certainly made sure his presence was felt. The riders thundered into the first turn and a clearly fired-up Owen rode a little over-zealously from the inside as he skittled Harrison, Jackson and teammate Bloomfield across the track. Jackson was clearly annoyed at hitting the deck for the second time and he stamped his feet in frustration. Somewhat tempering his mood, Newcastle's top man was excluded. In the rerun, the home duo were first from the gate and for two laps looked set for a crucial 5-1. But at the start of lap three, Harrison slowed dramatically to let Bloomfield through for a gift second place. Jackson took the win, with Harrison nursing his sick motor to third to leave the scores level at 12-12.

The following race saw Hunter and Scarisbrick make the early running, but in yet another hard-fought first turn the Fen Tigers bundled their way past the less-experienced Diamond. The Hunter soon became the hunted as the fiercely determined Baldwin made a huge effort to snatch the lead, almost driving inside the Aussie on the entry to the final lap. But the Newcastle number one held on to maintain the status quo.

Fen Tigers' Carl Baldwin.

Newcastle's other big gun, Owen, emerged for the following heat and, following the shenanigans of his first outing, the crowd gave him a less than warm welcome. However, the Diamonds' skipper was not top of the National League averages for no reason and he rode an immaculate race to hold off the wide-riding Knight, clocking the fastest time of the meeting – 54.6 seconds – in the process. Meanwhile Blackbird took third comfortably from the out-of-touch Barnsley.

In heat seven, Scarisbrick stepped in to take the rider replacement outing alongside Emerson against Harrison and Jackson. Yet another torrid opening lap ensued and Emerson clipped Jackson's back wheel – involved for the third time in a first turn incident that evening – and crashed heavily. Unfortunately it proved to be one too many knocks for the twenty-six-year-old's already fragile body and he was forced to pull out of the meeting with his shoulder heavily strapped. Bloomfield stepped into the breach, but could do little as Harrison won from Scarisbrick and Jackson to give Mildenhall the lead for the first time.

Heat eight brought together the opposing number twos and sevens. In the first running Farnham's enthusiasm got the better of him as he slid into the second-bend fencing while attempting to overtake Scarisbrick. In the rerun the young Diamond – who was proving to be such an adept performer at this level – made the gate. But Blackbird knew the track better and, although Scarisbrick left him little room by the fence, he roared through the gap to take the lead on the second lap much to the crowd's appreciation. Bloomfield took the free point in third.

In heat nine, Owen proved his class by leaving Henry and Baldwin well behind with Barnsley yet further back. In heat ten, the visitors' vulnerability was there for all to see as the Newcastle reserves emerged from the pits to cover Beaton's rider replacement ride and Emerson, their most recent addition to the casualty list. Knight and Blackbird were heavily favoured to score a 5-1; however, Knight lifted alarmingly at the start and found himself yards adrift at the first turn. But, showing real maturity, he did not panic and picked off Bloomfield at the end of the second lap and Barnsley at the start of the final lap, much to the relief of the home support.

Inevitably, with the gap now six points, the tactical substitute rule was applied and Owen was introduced to partner Hunter against Harrison and Farnham. Owen was the first to show but, surprisingly, it was Farnham who was second as they headed down the back straight having ridden a fine first turn. Desperate to join his partner at the front, Hunter made a big swoop around the second turn but, with Farnham also choosing the outside line, he was forced to go wider than intended. Harrison spotted an opportunity and scythed up the inside to take second. Hunter finally overcame Farnham on the final lap to salvage a 4-2, but the mischievous reserve had done a worthy job.

Heat twelve pitted Owen and Barnsley in against Baldwin and Knight. Although Knight put him under tremendous pressure for all four laps, once again the redoubtable Owen resisted him to take the win, but with Barnsley at the back no progress was made. A similar race followed as Hunter held off Harrison and Henry with Bloomfield at the rear. The visitors were looking over-reliant on their top two. On paper, heat fourteen looked crucial; with no Hunter or Owen present, Newcastle looked to Scarisbrick to get among the points. Jackson made the trap with the Newcastle number two on his tail. Mindful of Blackbird's move outside him earlier in the meeting Scarisbrick attempted to cover the move, but the exciting Fen Tiger outwitted him, driving inside him on the entry to the second lap. From then on in, the home side cruised to a 5-1 to go eight points clear with two races left. Jackson punched the air as he crossed the line, knowing that the home side only needed to avoid two consecutive 5-1 reverses to win the meeting.

However, the draw was still a strong possibility, particularly with Newcastle's big two likely to line-up in heats fifteen and sixteen. Sure enough, Hunter was drafted in as a tactical substitute in the penultimate race to partner Owen and, with the latter yet to take his rider replacement ride, there was little doubt that the dynamic duo would be joining forces again in the final heat.

Fen Tigers' skipper Henry and lynchpin Harrison stood in their way in heat fifteen, both desperate to split the visitors to guarantee the league points. Rising to the challenge it was Henry who showed in the early stages, but the sheer speed of the visitors saw them both roar past by the end of the first lap. To add injury to insult, the Mildenhall man smacked the fence on the final lap and ended up in an untidy heap badly bruised. And so, as with many of the clashes between the two sides, it came down to a last-heat decider.

Newcastle's Joe Owen, seen here in Ellesmere Port colours.

Such was the might of the Newcastle top two, that it was a somewhat fearful West Row faithful that greeted the riders as they rode round to the tapes for heat sixteen. Hunter would go from trap one, with Baldwin, Owen and Knight alongside him in that order, precisely the same line-up that had contested the critical race on Tyneside earlier in the season. Mindful of that reverse, hearts sank around the venue as the visitors emerged from the tapes in front and tore down the back straight together. But just before the Diamonds could sort out their team-riding formation, Knight saw his moment. The twenty-four-year-old grabbed a big handful of throttle around the third and fourth bends and just had the edge on Hunter as they entered the home straight, as the crowd screamed their approval. Try as he might, the Aussie could not respond and Knight held the crucial second place right through to the finish to clinch a narrow 49-47 victory for the Fen Tigers. At the race conclusion, his teammates poured through the pit gates and gave the Englishman the 'bumps', as is the tradition for any last-heat hero. It was a sweet result for the home team, not only 'getting one over' their big rivals, but putting them right back in title contention, just four points adrift with ten matches remaining. Ultimately though, it was not to be. Beaton's return to the saddle eased the burden on Owen and Hunter and they eventually won their second successive league crown by 51 points to Mildenhall's 48. Perhaps the crucial results in

The promising Carl Blackbird.

the run-in came at Hoddesdon, Rye House, where Mildenhall lost 45-51 and Newcastle won by the same score.

Thomas was bullish over the triumph. 'When they introduced the 45-point limit at the start of the season I heard one promoter say "that's it, now we've got Newcastle under control" but we showed them,' he said.

The season and indeed the West Row clash proved to be the end of an era as far as the rivalry was concerned. Newcastle tried their luck in the top division the following year, but it proved to be a disaster both financially and competitively as they finished bottom of the British League. Frustratingly for Mildenhall, they failed to exploit the absence of the Diamonds and were beaten to the 1984 National League title by unfashionable Long Eaton by a single point. When Newcastle eventually returned to the fold in 1986, they were under a different promotion and were a far less potent proposition. Success also waned for Mildenhall and, by 1989, the club were sixteenth in the National League, leading to their withdrawal from the league the following season. Thankfully, both clubs were re-established as regular speedway venues by the turn of the century.

Memories of evenings like the one described above can only act as an inspiration to Mildenhall and Newcastle. Though they were fierce rivals, that particular era will always be remembered with particular affection by supporters of both teams as being among the most exciting in their history.

14 August 1983: Mildenhall *v.* Newcastle: National League

MILDENHALL FEN TIGERS

		1	2	3	4	5	6	7	Total	BP
1	Richard Knight	3	2	2*	2	2	–	–	11	1
2	Carl Blackbird	0	1*	3	3	2*	–	–	9	2
3	Derek Harrison	1	3	2	2	1	–	–	9	–
4	Carl Baldwin	2	2	1*	1*	0	–	–	6	2
5	Robert Henry (Capt.)	1*	1*	2	1*	F	–	–	5	3
6	Dave Jackson (Res.)	FX	3	1	3	–	–	–	7	–
7	Ian Farnham (Res.)	2	FX	0	–	–	–	–	2	–

NEWCASTLE DIAMONDS

		1	2	3	4	5	6	7	Total	BP
1	Rod Hunter	2	3	3	1	3	3	1	16	–
2	Martin Scarisbrick	1*	0	2	2	1	–	–	6	1
3	Joe Owen (Capt.)	EX	3	3	3	3	2*	3	17	1
4	*Bobby Beaton R/R*	–	–	–	–	–	–	–	–	–
5	Alan Emerson	0	–	–	–	–	–	–	0	–
6	Neil Barnsley (Res.)	1	0	0	1	0	0	–	2	–
7	Laurie Bloomfield (Res.)	3	2	0	1*	0	0	–	6	1

Heat 1: Knight, Hunter, Scarisbrick, Blackbird, 54.8 secs

Heat 2 (twice rerun): Bloomfield, Farnham, Barnsley, Jackson (FX), 57.2 secs

Heat 3: Hunter, Baldwin, Henry, Emerson, 56.0 secs

Heat 4 (twice rerun): Jackson, Bloomfield, Harrison, Owen (EX), 55.0 secs

Heat 5: Hunter, Baldwin, Henry, Scarisbrick, 55.6 secs

Heat 6: Owen, Knight, Blackbird, Barnsley, 54.6 secs

Heat 7 (rerun): Harrison, Scarisbrick, Jackson, Bloomfield, 56.0 secs

Heat 8 (rerun): Blackbird, Scarisbrick, Bloomfield, Farnham (FX), 55.8 secs

Heat 9: Owen, Henry, Baldwin, Barnsley, 55.0 secs

Heat 10: Blackbird, Knight, Barnsley, Bloomfield, 55.8 secs

Heat 11: Owen, Harrison, Hunter, Farnham, 55.8 secs

Heat 12: Owen, Knight, Baldwin, Barnsley, 55.2 secs

Heat 13: Hunter, Harrison, Henry, Bloomfield, 56.0 secs

Heat 14: Jackson, Blackbird, Scarisbrick, Barnsley, 55.8 secs

Heat 15: Owen, Hunter, Harrison, Henry (F), 56.0 secs

Heat 16: Owen, Knight, Hunter, Baldwin, 55.6 secs

25 October 1993

Wolverhampton *v.* Belle Vue: Division One

1993 had been Sam Ermolenko's year. The flamboyant Californian was one of the most talented and exciting riders in the sport but, due in part to a series of injuries, had never quite managed to match his considerable ability with the achievements he was due, until now. Firstly he finally realised his dream by winning the World Individual Championship in Pocking, Germany on 29 August despite a controversial clash with Hans Nielsen. Then, just three weeks later, he led the USA to World Team Cup success at Coventry, once again getting the better of Nielsen and his fellow Danes. With his beloved Wolverhampton riding high at the top of Britain's Division One, it seemed nothing could go wrong for 'Sudden' Sam.

Evidently though, his nickname was not without reason and, on 17 October, he broke his leg in an innocuous-looking crash at Bradford and his season came to an abrupt halt. For 'Wolves' it was a huge blow. Seemingly coasting to the league title, they were now reduced to a mere shadow of the team that had put them fourteen points clear at one stage.

Dependable second-string Graham Jones, Sam's young sibling Charles Ermolenko and big-scoring little American Ronnie Correy were already on the long-term injured list when their star rider joined them. Without Jones, the younger Ermolenko and Correy the championship charge had lost much of its momentum, but the loss of Sam threatened to derail it completely. Not only was he the league's highest scoring rider, sitting on an eleven-point-plus average, but he was a superb skipper and an inspiration to his teammates. However, showing tremendous grit, a threadbare Wolves side – led by Swede Peter Karlsson, now in his fourth year with the club – just about stayed on track to win the title, despite dropping crucial points to Ipswich and Bradford. But Belle Vue began to smell blood and strung together a run of results to put them just three points behind the Midlanders but with a superior race points difference going into the final fixture of the season. Quite deliciously, the last match was Wolves *v.* the Aces at Monmore Green. If the Aces could win, they would take the two points available, plus the bonus point for beating Wolves on aggregate from the opposite fixture at home and pip them to the championship on race points. Wolves simply had to win or draw to take the spoils.

So, after thirty-nine meetings each, it all boiled down to one winner-takes-all shoot out for the league crown. A huge crowd of around 5,000 packed into the Ladbrooke Stadium for what promised to be a superb climax to the 1993 season. Spearheading the home side was Karlsson and fellow countryman Henrik Gustafsson, normally of King's Lynn, but stepping in as guest for Sam Ermolenko on this occasion. The unavailable Correy would be covered by the rider replacement facility. In support was the younger Karlsson brother Mikael, in his first season at Wolves, and experienced

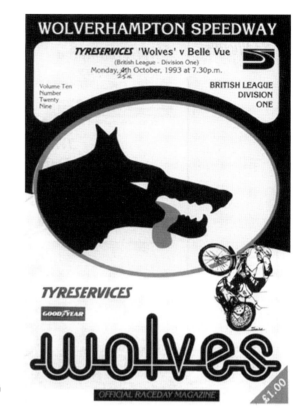

Right: Programme cover.

Below: Wolverhampton captain Sam Ermolenko.

Wolves guest Henrik Gustafsson.

former England internationals Gordon Kennett and Neil Evitts. The latter two were past their prime, however Kennett in particular was still capable of mixing it, even at the age of forty and his battling qualities had earned him something akin to cult status among the Wolves faithful. At reserve they tracked Stephen Morris, who was proving to be something of a trump card in the strange eight-man formula that was employed in 1993, and John Wainwright. The wily Peter Adams was the team manager.

The Aces fielded a more compact line-up, managed by John Hall. The experienced Shawn Moran captained a side that included fellow American Bobby Ott, Australian international Jason Lyons, English sensation Joe Screen and Carl Stonehewer, who had spent a year on loan at Monmore Green in 1990. They had their own injury troubles and their solid-scoring Dane Frede Schott, who had dislocated his shoulder in the previous week's home meeting against King's Lynn, would be covered by rider replacement. At reserve was Paul Smith, younger brother of England international Andy, and Max Schofield. The latter was really keyed up for the meeting, seeing it as a rare opportunity for some silverware. 'If I was in speedway for money, I'd starve. I don't make a living out of it – I have to work as well. But to win something like this would make it all worthwhile,' he said. Widely respected announcer Peter York was also excited at the enormity of the occasion. He said: 'I do British Finals and Commonwealth Finals that I thoroughly enjoy doing. But my heart is really in league racing and when you get a showdown on more or less the last night of the season, it's sensational.'

As the riders approached the tapes for heat one, the atmosphere was super-charged on the terraces with expectations high for a classic encounter. As they broke from the start it was Gustafsson who emerged in front, immediately proving that his guest status was not going to affect his appetite for the fray. Lyons was comfortable in second with the real action at the back. Aces' reserve Schofield, taking a rider replacement ride, overtook Kennett with a neat inside move on the first turn. But the forty-year-old former world number two was not for lying down and chased and harried until retaking third on the back straight of the third lap. Schofield responded by making an untidy attempt to cut back underneath on the next bend. It ended with Kennett being dumped on the track, looking very much the victim of some over-zealous tactics from his younger opponent. Surprisingly though, referee Graham Reeve saw nothing wrong in the move, excluded Kennett and awarded the heat as a 3-3.

Heat two brought together the Karlsson brothers against Screen and Stonehewer. 'Stoney' made the early running but a splendid outside move from Peter Karlsson saw him take over the lead in fine style at the start of the second lap. Screen, meanwhile, held third from the younger Karlsson until his machine ground to a halt on lap two, giving the home side a 4-2.

Heat three saw Kennett stepping in to take the first rider replacement ride for Ronnie Correy to partner Evitts, where they would face Ott and Moran. Ott made the break and was quickly in the clear with Kennett second. In third, Evitts dished out some rough treatment and looked to have taken Moran's front wheel away as he bit

The injured Ronny Correy.

Opposite: Belle Vue's hero Bobby Ott.

the dust on the exit of the first turn. However, referee Reeve once again saw nothing illegal and the race continued, finishing as a 3-3. The first of two reserves races was programmed for heat four. Perhaps surprisingly, it was the Aces duo of Smith and Schofield who scooted clear on the first turn with Wainwright sliding off. Morris set off in pursuit, but performed a 360-degree turn on the second lap to drop out of contention. The remounted Wainwright eventually took third behind the Aces duo, who had now given their team a two-point advantage.

In heat five, the Wolves partnership of Gustafsson and Kennett were first out of the traps. But, perhaps unaware it was his partner, Kennett squeezed the Swede out and let Joe Screen through. The nineteen-year-old England star scorched around the outside for a fine win to maintain the Aces' slender advantage. Rider replacement Peter Karlsson took his second successive win in heat six. Lyons was second and Evitts third for a Wolves 4-2 to level the match. Karlsson reappeared for the next heat to partner his younger brother against the Aces' American combination of Ott and Moran. In a tight first turn it was the elder of the two siblings who missed out as Mikael went clear. Though he was forced to take up the chase when twenty lengths in arrears, Peter made a bold effort and just failed to catch Moran on the line. Heat eight saw Kennett and Morris go in against Moran, taking his rider replacement ride, and Smith. The experienced Kennett made the gate and never looked like being caught but, with Morris falling for the second time that evening, it was another 3-3 and the scores were still level, locked at 24-24.

The stalemate continued in the next race. Mikael Karlsson took another impressive win and, although Evitts showed briefly, Screen and Stonehewer soon overtook him to fill the minor places. Gustafsson took the next race from Ott, but with Kennett bettering Moran for third Wolves took a narrow two-point lead. A superb 5-1 by the Karlsson boys in the next over Lyons and Stonehewer opened up the gap to six.

The Aces' response was to bring in Ott for a tactical substitute ride to partner Screen, and they duly cruised to a 5-1 over Wainwright and Evitts to slash the deficit to two. The same Aces pair emerged in heat thirteen to face somewhat stiffer opposition in the form of Peter Karlsson and Gustafsson. 'Henka' made the start and held off a strong challenge from Screen down the back straight. Left with a poor line on the next turn, Screen found himself relegated to last as Ott (outside) and Karlsson (inside) moved into second and third respectively. The Wolves fans then let out a mighty roar as Karlsson dived inside Ott on the next turn to set up a home 5-1.

The following heat saw Gustafsson back on track to partner Mikael Karlsson against Lyons and Stonehewer. Lyons was away first, but 'Henka' was hot on his trail and he swept by the Aussie at the end of the second lap. Meanwhile, Karlsson held off Stonehewer for a crucial third place point to put Wolves in a commanding eight-point

lead with just four heats left. Heat fifteen brought the second reserves race of the evening. Wainwright led around the first turn while Morris slid off for the third time during the meeting. Schofield and Smith pursued the lone Wolf and, looking far more accomplished, they were soon past. Wainwright too bit the dust on the last turn of the third lap and Morris, who had remounted, took over in third. However, at the race's conclusion the referee indicated that both Wolves were excluded, with Morris apparently having been given outside assistance from a member of the track staff, thus gifting the Aces an important 5-0.

With a mere three-point difference and just the three 'top-scorers' races remaining, tension was running high in the pits during the short interval, injured riders Jones, Correy and Schott all being on hand to encourage their teammates. Ermolenko unfortunately was still laid up in hospital and was kept in touch with proceedings via telephone. Jones admitted: 'I'm just as nervous as I would be if I was riding.'

Heat sixteen brought together Evitts and Wainwright against Moran and Schofield. To the acclaim of the home fans, the Wolves pairing were out of the traps first, but their joy was short-lived. Moran produced a smart cut-back on the back straight to go into the lead and Schofield nipped under Wainwright for third to give the Aces a 4-2 and, even more importantly, a one-point lead going into heat eighteen.

And so it all came down to the final race, just four laps to decide the 1993 Division One champions. Wolverhampton needed a 4-2 or better to win the meeting and the crucial two points that would give them the league title. Belle Vue needed a 3-3 or better to give them the two points plus the one bonus point to pinch the crown on race points difference. The men charged with the enormous responsibility were Gustafsson and Peter Karlsson for Wolves and Ott and Lyons for the Aces. Gustafsson had proven himself an able deputy for Sam Ermolenko, winning four of his five races, while Karlsson had accumulated two wins and two paid wins in his five outings. Ott had looked just about the most consistent of the Belle Vue contingent, gathering eleven points in his five rides, while Lyons had yet to win a heat, having scored seven from four.

As they approached the tapes, it is probably fair to say that Wolves were marginal favourites, with their twosome looking that bit sharper than the Aces pairing during the preceding heats. But in this situation, form was largely irrelevant; it was all about who would respond best under pressure. There was a collective intake of breath as the four bikes revved at the start for the race that would decide the league title. As they burst away it was Ott from gate two who had the slight edge. As they swung into the first turn, the American expertly leant on Karlsson, pinning him to the inside. Meanwhile, Lyons was riding an equally good bend and roared round the outside to join his teammate up front. The race was now well and truly on and if Wolves were to win the title, they would have to do it the hard way. Rather than team-riding, the Aces employed wise tactics; Ott rode off at high speed, opening up a decent lead while Lyons delayed Karlsson and Gustafsson at the back. Eventually, on the third bend of the third lap, the Wolves captain sliced underneath the Aussie and Gustafsson followed suit on the final lap. But by then it was too late as a fist-pumping Ott crossed the line for a 3-3, a one-point victory and the Division One title.

Aces' Aussie number one
Jason Lyons.

The Aces riders and management poured onto the track and gave the bumps to the final-heat heroes amid scenes of joy and despair from the opposing camps. After receiving the championship trophy, it was left to the ever-sporting Shawn Moran to pay tribute to the home side who, had they not been ravaged by injuries, would probably have claimed the title by then. 'Wolverhampton deserved it,' he said, 'but I can't see any better way to end the season, everything on the last race going for the league championship.'

He was right and it was the type of rare occasion in which everyone deserved credit. Despite their horrendous luck, Wolves had still managed to take the championship right down to the wire. They had gone down fighting. As for Belle Vue, they were given an unexpected chance to win the title and showed tremendous spirit, character and, indeed, bottle to seize the moment.

25 October 1993: Wolverhampton *v.* Belle Vue: Division One

WOLVERHAMPTON WOLVES

		1	2	3	4	5	6	Total	BP
1	Henrik Gustafsson (G)	3	1*	3	3	3	1*	14	2
2	Gordon Kennett	FX	2	2	3	1	0	8	–
3	Peter Karlsson (Capt.)	3	3	0	2*	2*	2	12	2
4	Mikael Karlsson	1	3	3	3	1	2	13	–
5	*Ronnie Correy R/R*	–	–	–	–	–	–	–	–
6	Neil Evitts	1*	1	0	0	2	–	4	1
7	Stephen Morris (Res.)	F	0	EX	–	–	–	0	–
8	John Wainwright (Res.)	1	1	FX	0	–	–	2	–

BELLE VUE ACES

		1	2	3	4	5	6	Total	BP
1	Jason Lyons	2	2	1	2	0	–	7	–
2	*Frede Schott R/R*	–	–	–	–	–	–	–	–
3	Joe Screen	EF	3	2	2*	0	3	10	1
4	Carl Stonehewer	2	0	1*	0	0	1	4	1
5	Bobby Ott	3	2	2	3	1	3	14	–
6	Shawn Moran (Capt.)	0	1*	2	0	3	–	6	1
7	Paul Smith (Res.)	3	0	1*	2*	–	–	6	2
8	Max Schofield (Res.)	1*	2*	3	1	–	–	7	2

Heat 1 (awarded): Gustafsson, Lyons, Schofield, Kennett (FX), no time

Heat 2: P Karlsson, Stonehewer, M Karlsson, Screen (EF), 59.9 secs

Heat 3: Ott, Kennett, Evitts, Moran, 60.8 secs

Heat 4: Smith, Schofield, Wainwright, Morris, 62.6 secs

Heat 5: Screen, Kennett, Gustafsson, Stonehewer, 60.3 secs

Heat 6: P Karlsson, Lyons, Evitts, Smith, 60.3 secs

Heat 7: M Karlsson, Ott, Moran, P Karlsson, 60.2 secs

Heat 8: Kennett, Moran, Smith, Morris, 60.8 secs

Heat 9: M Karlsson, Screen, Stonehewer, Evitts, 60.2 secs

Heat 10: Gustafsson, Ott, Kennett, Moran, 60.5 secs

Heat 11: M Karlsson, P Karlsson, Lyons, Stonehewer, 60.9 secs

Heat 12: Ott, Screen, Wainwright, Evitts, 61.1 secs

Heat 13: Gustafsson, P Karlsson, Ott, Screen, 60.1 secs

Heat 14: Gustafsson, Lyons, M Karlsson, Stonehewer, 61.0 secs

Heat 15 (awarded): Schofield, Smith, Wainwright (EX), Morris (EX), no time

Heat 16: Moran, Evitts, Schofield, Wainwright, 61.8 secs

Heat 17 (rerun): Screen, M Karlsson, Stonehewer, Kennett, 60.6 secs

Heat 18: Ott, P Karlsson, Gustafsson, Lyons, 60.3 secs

3 July 1999, Wroclaw

Grand Prix of Poland

There is no other country in the world that loves speedway quite as much as Poland. In 1973, the largest-ever crowd recorded at a meeting – 120,000 – crammed into Slaski Stadium, Katowice to watch home rider Jerzy Szczakiel create the biggest shock in the history of the sport by winning the World Individual Championship final. In Poland, speedway racing is ingrained in the culture. It is not unknown for regular league meetings to attract crowds of 20,000 or more. The riders are greeted and treated in a way that they are maybe not elsewhere in the world – like international sporting superstars.

During the 1990s and the early part of the twenty-first century, there were few stars that shone as brightly as Poland's own Tomasz Gollob. Quite simply, the boy from Bydgoszcz was pure magic on a motorbike. Lightning reflexes at the start, a superb eye for an overtaking opportunity and the courage to match, not to mention bags and bags of speed, in Poland he was worshipped as a god of the racetracks. In the 1990s and 2000s, there were fewer more spine-tingling moments than seeing Gollob taking on the rest of the world on home turf with what seemed like the whole of Poland cheering him on.

The hype, excitement and indeed expectation has probably never been higher than it was on Saturday 3 July 1999 when the World Championship Grand Prix Series arrived at the Olympic Stadium in Wroclaw. The twenty-eight-year-old Gollob was at the peak of his powers. He had finished third in the series in the previous two years and was now ready to mount his biggest challenge yet. Having won the Czech Grand Prix in Prague and consolidated with fifth place at the Swedish Grand Prix in Linkopping, he arrived at Wroclaw as the championship leader with 40 points. Next in line was the experienced Swede Jimmy Nilsen with 36 points. The chasing pack contained four riders who had already known what it felt like to be called world champion: Sweden's Tony Rickardsson, champion in 1994 and 1998, legendary Dane Hans Nielsen, champion in 1986, 1987, 1989, 1995 and American duo Billy Hamill and Greg Hancock, winners in 1996 and 1997 respectively. But with Gollob in such dynamic form for Bydgoszcz and Ipswich – his league clubs in Poland and Britain – and with two of the four remaining rounds to be ridden in his beloved Poland, surely this would be his year. Certainly the crowd thought so as over 20,000 of them arrived en masse with one simple wish – a Gollob victory. Unsurprisingly, he received a huge reception on the riders parade. But his army of admirers would have to be patient.

In the race formula used in 1999, the eight leading riders in the championship were seeded through to the main event that took place from heat eleven onwards. There, they would be joined by eight who emerged from the pre-main event scramble between the remaining sixteen riders. A place in the first two was all that mattered in

Left: Programme cover.

Opposite: Home favourite Tomasz Gollob.

every qualification heat right through to the semi-final. Anything less and you were either eliminated or facing elimination races.

Though they would be forced to wait for the main course, the crowd thoroughly enjoyed their appetiser, as Rafal Dobrucki and Robert Dados cruised to a Polish 1-2 in heat one. The ensuing heats also saw some rather tasty racing. For home fans, the sight of top contenders Hamill, Hancock and Britain's Mark Loram, winner of the previous round in Sweden, being eliminated only added to their hunger for a Gollob victory.

The masterful Nielsen, then thirty-nine, showed that he still had plenty of life in him by winning through to the next round in typically classy style. British duo Joe Screen and Chris Louis also eased through to the main event with fine rides. Emerging Australians Jason Crump and Ryan Sullivan would also join the big boys, the latter despite a tapes exclusion first time out. Swedish duo Mikael Karlsson and Henrik Gustafsson also did enough, while the leggy Dobrucki gave the crowd even more to cheer by making the cut.

The main event got underway with heat eleven, which saw Nilsen in the action for the first time. But perhaps not used to the track quite yet, he was caught out on the first turn, with Nielsen and Karlsson going either side of him to take the first two places.

Rickardsson rode a hard first turn in heat twelve, taking his opponents out wide. But Screen spotted the move and cleverly cut inside to take a fine win. In heat thirteen

Left: Jimmy Nilsen.

Opposite: The thirty-nine-year-old former world champion Hans Nielsen was still good enough to make the consolation final.

knowledge of track conditions again came to the fore when Gustafsson and Sullivan headed home the seeded Leigh Adams of Australia and Stefan Danno of Sweden.

Heat fourteen brought the moment the crowd had all been waiting for when Gollob emerged from the pits. A thunderous greeting welcomed him and he responded in the best way possible – with a lightening start. Looking super-fast, he stretched his lead lap after lap and finished with a huge 'wheelie' for an emphatic opening outing.

The crowd were still regathering their breath when the riders rolled to the tapes for heat fifteen, the first 'eliminator' race of the main event. With championship contender Nilsen in the line-up, there was plenty to interest the fans. Nerves got the better of Adams and he charged into the tapes and earned himself an exclusion and instant elimination from referee Steel. In the rerun, Nilsen rode a ruthless first turn, showing no comradeship whatsoever as he shoved Peter Karlsson aside. Czech Toni Kasper took advantage and claimed second spot, splitting the two Swedes to eliminate Karlsson.

The crowd were back on their feet in heat sixteen when Dobrucki pulled away to avoid elimination. Behind him, Danno rode a smart first turn to cut under Louis and Karger and send the latter two tumbling out of the meeting.

Although he was now into his fortieth year, heat seventeen proved that there was no sign of Nielsen mellowing in his old age. Despite not quite making the start from gate one, the Dane let his bike run straight into the first turn and effectively skittled Gustafsson, Rickardsson and Crump. The defending world champion came off worst from the nasty looking incident with his helmet colour and goggles flying off as he smashed into the fence at high-speed. Bravely, he dusted himself down and, after a trip to the medical room, emerged for the rerun, where the referee – perhaps surprisingly – had allowed all four back for the rerun. This time Nielsen made a clear break. But with a full-blooded effort around the outside, it was Gustafsson who took the lead down the back straight. Both riders went out wide for the dirt on turns three and four and, as they did, Crump took advantage. A crafty burst up the inside took him from third to first as they entered the second lap and, with Gustafsson pinned on the fence, Nielsen also took his opportunity to retake second place. After the frantic first lap, they settled into their positions with Crump and Nielsen progressing straight to the semi-finals with Gustafsson and an understandably jaded-looking Rickardsson facing elimination heats next time out.

With Gollob out next there was a buzz about the stadium as he too sought to clinch his place in the semis. Facing him were Sullivan, Screen and Mikael Karlsson. From the inside it was the twenty-three-year-old Aussie who made the jump. Behind him Gollob bucked and reared on the first turn, but managed to get it under control to follow Sullivan home for the crucial second place.

Heat nineteen was an all-Swedish affair featuring Nilsen, Danno, Gustafsson and Mikael Karlsson. Having witnessed the grip the likes of Gollob, Dobrucki and Nielsen had found on the outside, the wily Nilsen was not about to fall for that trick. Starting from gate one, he moved across the track to block the efforts of Gustafsson and Karlsson. Danno duly exploited the gap and went on to take the win, while Nilsen's first-turn tactics ultimately rewarded him with second place and condemned his countrymen to elimination.

The semi-final line-up would be completed by the first two home in heat twenty. From the outside, Rickardsson made a fine getaway and – considering his first turn difficulties earlier in evening – summoned great courage to cut across the field. Dobrucki showed briefly in second. But impressive track-craft from Screen silenced the home supporters as he scooted underneath the Pole to claim the crucial position. The twenty-six-year-old Brit then set out after the clearly vulnerable Rickardsson but, despite applying some pressure he was content to simply qualify. Dobrucki and Kasper, who was never in contention, were now out.

The first semi-final brought out Gollob – the man the fans were here to see – against Danno, Crump and Screen. The Pole actually made the start from the inside, but left no-one in any doubt where he really wanted to be, scraping the fence on the outside. He willingly gave ground and allowed Danno and Crump to cut under him as grabbed a huge handful of throttle and roared around the outside. The three riders arrived at the back straight together and it was pretty clear that at least one of them would have to give ground. It certainly wasn't going to be the adrenaline-fuelled Pole as he screamed through at full speed. Stuck in the middle, it was Crump who felt the squeeze and had to back off. Danno, producing the best form of his career, rode a fine line to follow Gollob all the way to the finish line. A deafening roar greeted the result, but for Crump and Screen there was little to shout about. Both were consigned to the consolation final.

The second semi-final was equally dramatic, but for different reasons. Rickardsson scorched away from gate three to lead round the first bend. Behind him Nielsen produced a fine surge to go around Sullivan, with Nilsen rooted at the back. But, as they tore into the third turn, Nielsen lifted and missed the corner, allowing the Aussie to retake second place. That was how it stayed for the next two laps, until Sullivan inexplicably came off entering the third turn. The referee stopped the race and called a rerun. It was more than a trifle fortunate for Nilsen who was way at the back at the time of the stoppage. Nonetheless, as so often happens in cases like this, the Swede was first out of the traps in the rerun. Behind him Rickardsson was gaining a measure of revenge on his earlier clash with Nielsen by shutting the door firmly in his face on the back straight. Looking back to his normal self, the world champion chased after Nilsen and swept underneath him in fine style on the third lap. His fellow countryman was

The top British rider in Wroclaw was Joe Screen.

riding somewhat conservatively and seemed content just to grab one of the two available final berths, which he duly did.

With his pride hurt, Nielsen made little impact in the consolation final as the young guns fought it out. Rounding off a fine evening, Screen made maximum use of the grip out by the boards to drive round Sullivan and Crump in spectacular style. It was good speedway, but for the fans it was little more than killing time. For, next up, was the main final, starring – as far they were concerned – national hero Tomasz Gollob. Up against him were three Swedes – current world number one Rickardsson, Nilsen, who was lying second in the championship standings and Danno, the surprise packet. As part of the 'showbiz' element of the Grand Prix Series the organisers had the finalists strut out to the start line to select their gate positions. The crowd lapped up the theatre of it all. Gollob, who had the first pick, surprised no-one by selecting gate four. Rickardsson, as winner of the other semi-final took gate three, Danno took gate one and Nilsen was left with gate two. For Nilsen, fourth choice proved to be no handicap though, as he made a tremendous start to lead around the first turn. Gollob, meanwhile, strained his way around Rickardsson and Danno to move to second. Of course, there was never any chance of the Pole settling for second and he set off in hot pursuit of Nilsen. However, despite looking a little sluggish earlier on, the thirty-two-year-old Swede had obviously reserved his best for last. Riding faster than he had all night, he held Gollob at bay rather comfortably for three laps. But as they entered the final circuit, the daring Gollob launched his bike into the first and second turns and drew within a bike length on the back straight. With the crowd going crazy, he sensationally hurtled underneath Nilsen on entry to the third turn. But, at the speed he was travelling, he could not hold the line and he went far too wide, almost whacking the fence as Nilsen retook the initiative on the inside.

Gollob managed to get his wheels in line quickly and contorted himself into an aerodynamic position for the dash to the flag. With the crowd at fever pitch the two riders motored to the line neck and neck. Possessing a fraction more speed, Gollob just managed to edge ahead and crossed the line just half-a-length ahead. Cue party-time in Wroclaw. Flares were set off, drums were banged, and ticker tape was thrown into the air as the terraces danced ecstatically. Ever the showman, Gollob milked the crowd's adulation, treating them to a set of huge 'wheelies' and taking the Polish flag on a lap of honour. Commenting on the incredible final race, Nilsen said: 'I knew Tomasz was there and I knew he was quick. I just tried to ride my own line and see what he could do. But I know he can light a fuse right now and again so I kept looking back to see what he was up to. I could hear on the last corner he was coming in and he wasn't going to shut off. So I thought "I'm shutting off here because I still want to be alive tomorrow". And then I nearly came back because he almost hit the fence. So it was good speedway with a close finish again.'

The result left Gollob nine points clear of Nilsen in the title race, with Rickardsson a massive twenty-four adrift. With just three rounds remaining, including one at his beloved home track of Bydgoszcz, few would have bet against Gollob going on to take the gold medal. But, perhaps weighed down by the expectation of a nation, he could not quite deliver. He failed to reach the final at any of the remaining GPs and, with Rickardsson winning two and finishing runner-up in the other, the Swede hung onto his title with Gollob having to settle for silver. The Pole looks destined to become one of the most talented riders never to be world champion. But he has left an indelible mark on the sport, as anyone who has witnessed the sheer atmosphere and excitement generated by Gollob in full flight in front of his home fans will testify.

Grand Prix of Poland Wroclaw, Poland 3 July 1999

SCORECHART:

Tomasz Gollob (Poland), 25 points; Jimmy Nilsen (Sweden), 20; Stefan Danno (Sweden), 18; Tony Rickardsson (Sweden), 16; Joe Screen (Great Britain), 15; Ryan Sullivan (Australia), 14; Jason Crump (Australia), 12; Hans Nielsen (Denmark), 10; Mikael Karlsson (Sweden), 8; Rafal Dobrucki (Poland), 8; Toni Kasper (Czech Republic), 7; Henrik Gustafsson (Sweden), 7; Brian Karger (Denmark), 6; Peter Karlsson (Sweden), 6; Chris Louis (Great Britain), 5; Leigh Adams (Australia), 5; Greg Hancock (USA), 4; Robert Dados (Poland), 4; John Jorgensen (Denmark), 3; Billy Hamill (USA), 3; Brian Andersen (Denmark), 2; Mark Loram (Great Britain), 2; Mario Jirout (Czech Republic), 1; Andy Smith (Great Britain), 1.

PRE-MAIN EVENT:

Heat 1: Dobrucki, Dados, Jorgensen, Sullivan (EX), 66.5 secs

Heat 2: Hancock, Screen, Hamill, Loram, 66.4 secs

Heat 3: Crump, M Karlsson, Jirout, Andersen (F), 66.3 secs

Heat 4: Louis, Nielsen, Smith, Gustafsson, 67.1 secs

Heat 5: Gustafsson, Jorgensen, *Loram*, *Jirout*, 67.2 secs

Heat 6: Sullivan, Hamill, *Andersen*, *Smith (EX)*, 66.7 secs

Heat 7: Nielsen, Screen, Crump, Dobrucki, 66.7 secs

Heat 8: Louis, M Karlsson, Hancock, Dados, 67.0 secs

Heat 9: Gustafsson, Crump, *Dados*, *Hamill*, 66.8 secs

Heat 10: Dobrucki, Sullivan, *Hancock*, *Jorgensen*, 67.4 secs

MAIN EVENT:

Heat 11: Nielsen, M Karlsson, Nilsen, Karger, 67.3 secs

Heat 12: Screen, Rickardsson, Louis, Kasper, 66.6 secs

Heat 13: Gustafsson, Sullivan, Adams, Danno, 67.1 secs

Heat 14: Gollob, Crump, Dobrucki, P Karlsson, 66.8 secs

Heat 15: Nilsen, Kasper, *P Karlsson*, *Adams (EX)*, 67.6 secs

Heat 16: Dobrucki, Danno, *Karger*, *Louis*, 67.4 secs

Heat 17 (rerun): Crump, Nielsen, Gustafsson, Rickardsson (RET.), 66.6 secs

Heat 18: Sullivan, Gollob, Screen, M Karlsson, 67.4 secs

Heat 19: Danno, Nilsen, *M Karlsson*, *Gustafsson*, 67.8 secs

Heat 20: Rickardsson, Screen, *Dobrucki*, *Kasper*, 67.4 secs

FINAL EVENT:

Semi-final 1: Gollob, Danno, Crump, Screen (RET.), 67.1 secs

Semi-final 2 (rerun): Rickardsson, Nilen, Nielsen, Sullivan (FX), 68.1 secs

Consolation final: Screen, Sullivan, Crump, Nielsen, 67.4 secs

Final: Gollob, Nilsen, Danno, Rickardsson, secs

Italics denote elimination

25 October 2003

Coventry *v.* Poole: Elite League Knock Out Cup Final Second Leg

League speedway in Britain has gone through what seems like endless reinvention during its varied history. Northern League, Southern League, Provincial League, National League, British League, Premier League, Elite League... the list goes on and on. Not to mention the formats: one big league, regional splits, divisions and, in the early part of the twenty-first century, a play-off system.

Throughout the ever-changing league competitions, the concept of a Knock-Out (KO) Cup has endured largely unchanged since the first cup competition, the English Dirt Track Knock-Out Cup, in 1929. The straightforward nature of the cup is probably what has given it its longevity. Teams are drawn out randomly to compete against another team in a two-legged tie; the winners go though to the next round, the losers are out. The KO Cup has given supporters in the UK some of its most exciting speedway. Its all-or-nothing format appeals to the fans and its prestige is unquestioned.

In 2003, two of the most famous names in British speedway history – Coventry Bees and Poole Pirates – clashed in the Elite League KO Cup final. As ever it was an eagerly awaited confrontation. Both sides were packed with some of the sport's leading international stars and, as well as the glory of winning the cup, there was extra incentive for both sides to succeed. Coventry were still smarting after Poole had beaten them in the two-legged grand final play-off to claim the league championships and saw the cup as an ideal opportunity for revenge. Surprisingly, they had also not tasted KO Cup final success since 1967. The Pirates' cup record was even worse, having never actually won the cup in top-flight speedway, and consequently had never done the 'double' at this level.

For their current crop of riders, this was a chance to etch their names into the club's history books. It certainly was a mighty team that the champions called upon for both legs of the 2003 KO Cup final. Captained by Swedish multi-world champion Tony Rickardsson, they fielded Australian Leigh Adams, one of the highest-scoring riders in British league history, Danish international Bjarne Pedersen, 2000 world champion Mark Loram – a former Pirate – as guest for Czech sensation Lukas Dryml, elder brother Ales Dryml jnr, exciting Brazilian-born Swede Antonio Lindback and battling Yorkshireman Gary Stead. It was a power-packed line-up with a stupendous spearhead and no obvious weak link. Coventry were no mugs though – as an early season victory at Poole's Wimborne Road Stadium proved – and had the riders to give the champions a real test. Britain's Lee Richardson and Sweden's Andreas Jonsson were two of the hottest properties in world speedway. They were supported by the rapidly improving American duo Billy Janniro and Ryan Fisher and no-frills Englishmen Stuart Robson and Jason Bunyan. Their skipper, former world champion Billy Hamill would be

Programme cover.

covered by the rider replacement facility in the first leg and by guest Mikael Max of Wolverhampton in the second.

Following their comfortable victory over the Bees in the league play-off, Poole went into the final as warm favourites. But, following a spirited showing by Coventry in the first leg in Dorset, where superstar duo Rickardsson and Adams just about dragged their team to a 46-42 win, the outcome was very much in the balance as the teams looked towards the second leg due to take place at Brandon Stadium two nights later.

The Bees had been buoyed by the form of Richardson, who had taken points off Poole's top two, and by the showings of Americans Janniro and Fisher, who had contributed a fine 22-point haul between them. With only four points to make up, the home fans were confident that their heroes could salvage some silverware for the season, particularly on their own patch. But before the men and their machines could sort out who were to be the cup winners, nature had its say in proceedings. In the hours building up to the meeting, heavy showers battered down on the Coventry track, rendering one of the smoothest and safest surfaces in the country a virtual

Opposite: Coventry's exciting Swede Andreas Jonsson.

Right: Antonio Lindback.

quagmire. Nevertheless, with Poole's riders particularly unhappy with conditions, referee Jim Lawrence ruled the meeting could go ahead with the rain still beating down. Within three races, the Pirates' four-point advantage had been wiped out as Coventry took a 12-6 lead to go two up on aggregate.

Richardson had repeated his heat one victory over Adams from the first leg. Fisher and Bunyan then took a 4-2 in the reserves race followed by a Janniro/Max 5-1 in heat three. The latter race provided evidence of how tricky track conditions were as Loram, a rider of huge experience and skill, struggled to control his machine as he slipped from second to fourth on the first lap. Seeing Rickardsson struggling at the back in the next only served to reinforce some riders' contention that the meeting should be postponed. But, with Jonsson and Fisher taking a 5-1 up front, Coventry manager Colin Pratt was happy to continue, with the 17-7 scoreline now translating into a six-point lead overall.

The situation was compounded yet further – as far as the Pirates were concerned – in the next heat. Pedersen was excluded from the first running after losing control on the first turn, causing Janniro to crash. Then, in the rerun, Adams was left at the start as Janniro and Max took Coventry's third successive 5-1. Two more 4-2s followed in heat six and heat seven, with the home riders looking far more determined than their visitors. With the scores standing at 30-18, the Bees were now sitting on a 14-point cushion on aggregate, with the cup looking well set for the Midlands club. However, the rain had now stopped and the track began to dry out. Although it may not have been quite to the Poole riders' taste, it was certainly more palatable and in the ensuing races they began to show much more appetite for the fray.

Poole team manager Neil Middleditch pitched Adams in as a tactical substitute in the next race and, with partner Pedersen making the start, they teamed up for a 5-1 to try and kick-start some sort of fightback. Rickardsson sprang into life in winning the next two heats, a welcome sight for Poole fans. But with his respective partners Dryml and Loram both trailing at the back, the heats were levelled and the league champions were still ten points in arrears with just five heats remaining.

Adams and Pedersen emerged for heat eleven, desperate to make inroads into the Coventry lead, with Jonsson and Bunyan in opposition. The Poole duo made the start but, with the daring Jonsson on their tails, they could not relax and, sure enough, the determined Swede split them as they completed the first lap to restrict them to a 4-2.

Pedersen re-emerged for the following heat, in as a tactical substitute for Dryml, as Middleditch tried everything to drag his side back into contention. Max gated but made a dreadful error on the first turn, allowing both Poole riders through. Fisher salvaged the situation somewhat by slipping inside Loram as they entered the second lap. But with a mud-splattered Max at the rear, the overall deficit had now been brought down to a more workable six. With the travelling band of Poole supporters now warming to the occasion, there was real tension in the atmosphere as Coventry fans sensed that the trophy that had looked all but won five races earlier was still far from guaranteed. Heat thirteen would be crucial.

Both teams' big guns lined up at the start, Richardson and Jonsson for Coventry, Rickardsson and Adams for Poole. A 5-1 for the home side would virtually clinch the cup, meaning Poole would need two 5-0s to draw. But from the tapes it was Adams and Rickardsson who emerged first to keep the match well and truly alive. As they headed down the back straight, it was Jonsson who moved up to challenge. As they tore into the third bend, the young Swede somehow managed to find a way between the team-riding duo to take the lead. It was an audacious move equal in its bravery and brilliance and he went on to take a well-deserved win, much to the delight of the home supporters.

The penultimate race saw Janniro and Fisher line up against Lindback and Stead – both of whom had to yet to take their minimum of three rides. With the home duo having accumulated sixteen points to their opponents' two until this stage, the game looked up for Poole. But fate was about to take an unexpected twist. As they battled round the first turn, Fisher – on the inside – lifted alarmingly and speared Lindback, who in turn sent Janniro slamming into the fence. Fisher was the obvious cause of the stoppage and was promptly excluded by referee Lawrence. Lindback remained on the

Poole's legendary Swede Tony Rickardsson.

deck for sometime and, as he lay there, frantic action was also taking place in the pits, where Janniro's pit crew had to prepare a second machine for the rerun, after the crash had wrecked his first machine. Poole's young Swede was eventually declared unfit to continue, meaning Dryml would step in as replacement. But, in a rather crafty and controversial interpretation of the rules, Middleditch introduced Loram as a tactical substitute instead of Dryml. Effectively, Lindback had now had his third recorded ride and the move was therefore perfectly legitimate. With the crowd now extremely vocal, the riders lined up for the rerun. Stead was the surprise first arrival at the first turn with Loram and Janniro behind him in that order. But the Pirates got in each other's way, allowing Janniro to take the initiative down the back straight. Looking quite uncomfortable, the American got out of shape entering the third turn, allowing both visitors to steam under him as he fell. He remounted to take third place, but what should have been a cup-clinching race had now set up a last-heat decider. The 4,500 crowd were now at fever pitch as Coventry opted for Richardson and Jonsson and Poole went for Rickardsson and Adams.

A 3-3 or better would do for Coventry, a 4-2 for Poole would mean a draw and a two-legged replay, while a 5-1 for the visitors would clinch a miraculous comeback. From the tapes it was Adams who took the lead with Jonsson in his tyre tracks on the first turn. Eyeing the situation up, Rickardsson turned his bike expertly and drove hard under Jonsson on the second turn to move onto his partner's shoulder. With the small pocket of Poole fans going crazy, in an otherwise silenced stadium, the Pirates rode a faultless four laps to take the 5-1, the cup and a famous double. Afterwards, the overriding emotion was disbelief, from both camps. Coventry boss Pratt said: 'I am gutted, and as a manager it must go down as one of the biggest disappointments of my career. I am a bit disillusioned by it all, as we have done everything but win it, and Lady Luck just wasn't with us when we needed her.' He was however, more than a little perturbed by the events of the penultimate race. 'It was a bit of a fiasco that Antonio Lindback was declared unfit to ride, yet was jumping up and down cheering in the pits.' However, he also sportingly admitted: 'It is difficult to explain what went wrong. The boys gave it their best shot but in the end we were beaten by a better team.' Poole skipper Rickardsson, a man of vast experience was equally incredulous. Afterwards, he said: 'I'm still pinching myself that we won. In fact, I'm still asking myself "did this really happen?" What a night this has been. It has been so difficult for the riders. I thought the track was too dangerous to ride. All of the rest of the boys thought so too – as long as it was raining we shouldn't have been out there. But Coventry had a good lead and saw an opportunity to beat us. We backed off a bit early on and it was only the Coventry boys racing. Then with two races to go we realised we could win it. We were down and out after seven races. Even if we had got up I never thought we could pull it back. I have probably been in a meeting like this where we have been that far behind and still won but certainly not a showpiece occasion like this, in a cup final.'

Last-heat hero Leigh Adams.

25 October 2003: Coventry *v.* Poole: Elite League Cup Final Second Leg

COVENTRY BEES

		1	2	3	4	5	6	7	Total	BP
1	Lee Richardson (Capt.)	3	3	1*	R	0	–	–	7	1
2	Stuart Robson	0	1	R	–	–	–	–	1	–
3	Mikael Max	2*	3	2	0	–	–	–	7	1
4	Billy Janniro	3	2*	1*	1	–	–	–	7	2
5	Andreas Jonsson	3	3	2	3	1	–	–	12	–
6	Jason Bunyan (Res.)	1	1	0	–	–	–	–	2	–
7	Ryan Fisher (Res.)	3	2*	1	2	2	X	–	10	1

POOLE PIRATES

		1	2	3	4	5	6	7	Total	BP
1	Leigh Adams	2	1	2*	3	1*	3	–	12	2
2	Bjarne Pedersen	1*	X	3	1	3	–	–	8	1
3	Mark Loram	R	2	0	1	3	–	–	6	–
4	Antonio Lindback	1	0	N	–	–	–	–	1	–
5	Tony Rickardsson (Capt.)	0	2	3	3	2	2*	–	12	1
6	Ales Dryml (Res.)	2	R	0	–	–	–	–	2	–
7	Gary Stead (Res.)	F	1	2*	–	–	–	–	3	1

Heat 1: Richardson, Adams, Pedersen, Robson, 60.5 secs

Heat 2: Fisher, Dryml, Bunyan, Stead (F), 61.7 secs

Heat 3: Janniro, Max, Lindback, Loram (RET.), 63.2 secs

Heat 4: Jonsson, Fisher, Stead, Rickardsson, 63.4 secs

Heat 5 (rerun): Max, Janniro, Adams, Pedersen (FX), 61.2 secs

Heat 6: Richardson, Rickardsson, Robson, Dryml (RET.), 62.0 secs

Heat 7: Jonsson, Loram, Bunyan, Lindback, 62.3 secs

Heat 8: Pedersen, Adams, Fisher, Robson (RET.), 62.4 secs

Heat 9: Rickardsson, Max, Janniro, Dryml, 60.3 secs

Heat 10: Rickardsson, Fisher, Richardson, Loram, 61.6 secs

Heat 11: Adams, Jonsson, Pedersen, Bunyan, 62.0 secs

Heat 12: Pedersen, Fisher, Loram, Max, 62.2 secs

Heat 13: Jonsson, Rickardsson, Adams, Richardson (RET.), 61.4 secs

Heat 14 (rerun): Loram, Stead, Janniro (F), Fisher (FX), Lindback (FN), 63.1 secs

Heat 15: Adams, Rickardsson, Jonsson, Richardson, 63.0 secs

7 August 2004, Poole

World Cup Final

International speedway team events suffered something of a turbulent period during the late 1980s and 1990s, as interest in this particular area of the sport waned. It is unclear exactly why this was, but the constant toying with the formula of the World Team Cup and World Pairs Championships, eventually leading to the merger of the two competitions by the sport's authorities, certainly did not help. However, in 2001, a brand new competition was unveiled – the Speedway World Cup. Unlike previous incarnations, this championship would be hosted by a single country on a week-long basis, helping to generate a much greater sense of occasion. Following a successful first three years of the championship, the event arrived in Great Britain in 2004, firmly established as one of the annual highlights of the international speedway calendar. Blessed with fine weather, crowds flocked to the qualifying meetings at Eastbourne and Poole for some fantastic racing between the world's leading speedway nations. With the host country qualifying from their round at Eastbourne in such impressive style, it was an excited home crowd that trooped into Poole's Wimborne Road Stadium for the final on Saturday 7 August.

A British side had not won the World Team Championship since 1989, when England triumphed at Bradford. But, hopes were high for a solid quintet consisting of 2000 world champion Mark Loram, the world-class Scott Nicholls and Lee Richardson, 1992 world champion Gary Havelock and the rejuvenated David Norris. Standing in their way were defending champions Sweden, Denmark and Poland. Surprisingly, pre-tournament favourites Australia were eliminated in the race-off meeting, after Polish hero Tomasz Gollob produced a thrilling overtaking of Aussie superstar Jason Crump in the final heat. Sweden tracked modern great Tony Rickardsson, the experienced brothers Peter Karlsson and Mikael Max, the exciting Andreas Jonsson and the precocious nineteen-year-old Antonio Lindback. Denmark had the defending World Champion Nicki Pedersen, established internationals Hans Andersen and Bjarne Pedersen and emerging talents Kenneth Bjerre and Niels-Kristian Iversen. The outsiders were Poland, with their iconic captain Gollob heading up an inexperienced group of riders including Jarek Hampel, Krzysztof Kasprzak, Janusz Kolodziej and Marcin Rempala. However, after upsetting Australia just two nights earlier on the same track, no-one was underestimating them.

The packed terraces though were dominated by Union Jack flags and, as the riders emerged from the pits for heat one, hundreds of air horns were blasted to herald the arrival of GB's David Norris. With the hype at fever pitch, both off and on-track, it was little surprise that the first piece of action should result in a fall. After a tight first bend, Hans Andersen was left spreadeagled on the track. Referee Mick Bates allowed all four back and the Dane took full advantage, shooting from the start to record a

Programme cover.

tapes-to-flag win. Mikael Max took two points for Sweden, with Norris having to pick his way past Poland's Kasprzak to take one for GB.

Heat two saw the multiple world champion Rickardsson showing his class. Hampel burst away from the field to establish an early lead and was cruising with two laps gone. But the mighty Swede reeled him in and bluffed the young Pole on the final turn into going wide as he cut inside him to take the victory by a wheel. Richardson was third for GB with Nicki Pedersen surprisingly struggling at the back.

Mark Loram emerged for GB in heat three and, after a scorching 15-point maximum at the qualifying round in Eastbourne, much was expected of the thirty-three-year-old. He duly delivered, streaking from the tapes to secure a confident win, much to the delight of the crowd. Bjerre, Lindback and Gollob followed him in that order. In the following heat, GB skipper Nicholls gave the fans even more to shout about as he left the others for dead to log a fine win.

Heat five had to be rerun after Karlsson crashed on the first lap following a rash dive into the third turn, which left him tucked under the air fence. The second attempt produced the third successive win for GB with Havelock riding an excellent first lap to take command ahead of Rempala and Bjarne Pedersen.

So, after the first round of five heats, the crowd had even more reason to be excited, with the home team leading with eleven points, the Swedes having seven and the Poles

Carrying the hopes of a nation: Scott
Nicholls and Lee Richardson.

and Danes both on six. But the response was swift. Lindback, Karlsson and Rickardsson all recorded wins for Sweden in the next round of heats. In the latter's race win in heat seven, GB's Nicholls could count himself lucky to not be excluded after appearing to spear Bjarne Pedersen into the fence, before referee Mick Bates allowed all four into the rerun. But there was also a morale-boosting victory by Norris, who saw off the big guns of Nicki Pedersen, Jonsson and Gollob in heat nine. So, after heat ten, Sweden and GB were locked on eighteen points, the Danes were poised on sixteen with the Poles losing touch on eight.

The following heat saw GB skipper Nicholls in the thick of the action again. He battled past Bjerre and was just a machine length behind Max at the finish. Sweden's top man Rickardsson logged another routine win in heat twelve, his third in succession.

Heat thirteen saw the first use of the 'Joker' rule, whereby a team six points in arrears can nominate a rider whose points will score double in that race. Each team was only permitted to use the rule once per meeting. Bjarne Pedersen bore the responsibility for Denmark. The first attempt to race was halted after Pedersen anticipated rather than reacted to the tapes rising, so referee Bates pulled them back, calling it an unsatisfactory start. In the restart the Dane was not so swift as GB's Norris scorched away from gate two and on to a fine win. Polish spoiler Kolodziej, rode a splendid first lap

Dane Hans Andersen upset many British supporters.

to earn second. Meanwhile, Pedersen squeezed past Lindback for a disappointing third, earning Denmark a mere two points from their tactical move.

Heat fourteen was a real cracker. Andersen led in the early stages, but was passed by Richardson, then by Jonsson. The twenty-three-year-old Swede, never one to settle for second, then set after Richardson with real vigour. Dramatically, he swept under him on the third lap back straight. But, in a superb counter-punch, Richardson rode hard with the Swede into the next turn before cleverly cutting back underneath to retake the lead and go on to take a hard-fought win.

Karlsson trapped on Loram in heat fifteen and rode a faultless four laps for the win. The meeting had now turned into a two-horse race. GB headed the leaderboard on 30 points, just a single point ahead of Sweden. The Danes were back on 22, with the Poles completely out of it on ten.

GB cranked up the pressure by taking maximum points from the next two heats. Firstly Richardson won heat sixteen with a tapes-to-flag effort. Then Loram triumphed in heat seventeen. Crucially, Rickardsson was at the back behind Andersen and Kolodziej.

With the gap at six, Sweden had an opportunity to play the 'Joker', but team manager Tony Olsson decided to keep it in hand with the inexperienced Lindback out next. He may well have regretted it afterwards as the nineteen-year-old swept to an impressive victory. But it was behind the youngster where the real drama lay. After scrapping his way past Nicki Pedersen for third place, Nicholls inexplicably shut off his machine and pulled to one side as they entered the final lap. It emerged that the GB skipper had seen a red light – most probably from a camera in the crowd – and thought the referee had stopped the race. Despite protests from the GB camp, the referee had little option but to let the result stand. And so the gap was halved to three; a crucial point lost perhaps?

David Norris, one of England's heroes on the night.

After the ridiculous came the sublime as the crowd were served up a real treat in heat nineteen. Andersen took the lead from Havelock on the first lap, who then had to ward off the close attentions of Jonsson. Suddenly, on the second lap, the young Pole Rempala cut through from fourth to second. From there to the finish he and Havelock passed and repassed with the Pole dashing down the straights, but leaving huge gaps on the corners. With the crowd in a frenzy, Rempala led into the final turn with Havelock hugging the inside to retake second spot. This time though, the Brit rode a clever line towards the chequered flag, leaving the Pole with no way through and clinching two points. With Jonsson at the back, the gap was now five. But with another Karlsson heat victory and Norris back in third, Sweden reapplied the pressure in heat twenty.

Heat twenty-one saw Havelock produce another memorable manoeuvre. Starting from the difficult gate four, he was last away, but was first to the back straight after a majestic cut-back. But a rerun was called after Nicki Pedersen lost control on lap two and hurtled across the track where he collected Max, and the two of them were left in an untidy heap of men and machines. Red lights came on and Pedersen was excluded. Max took his time to gather his senses, but took his place in the rerun where he bravely finished second to Kolodziej, with Havelock pressing in third, probably cursing his misfortune.

Heat twenty-two saw Rickardsson register his fourth win of the evening. With Norris back in third, the scores were now level at 41 points each and the atmosphere was electric.

The next race brought yet more controversy, Lindback was away and clear when, on the second lap, Kolodziej locked up and lost control, balking a closely placed Richardson who was forced to pull to one side. The referee stopped the race and excluded the Pole. The Swedes protested, arguing quite legitimately that no-one had actually fallen and therefore there was no need for the race to be stopped. However, the

The underrated Peter Karlsson of Sweden.

decision stood and Richardson was given a second bite at the cherry. He duly gobbled it, making a great start from gate three to lead all the way, with Lindback back in second. Advantage Great Britain. The tension was now palpable as Loram, Jonsson, Bjarne Pedersen and Hampel lined up for the penultimate race. Jonsson just made the jump, but Loram was right on his exhaust pipe. The Brit rode a typically whole-hearted race, stalking the Swede every inch of the way, almost clipping his back wheel on at least a couple of occasions. But with the track becoming increasingly bare, grip was hard to find and the Swede rode an intelligent line to hold on by a bike's length at the finish.

So, after ninety-nine races of World Cup speedway that week, the most important one would be the last one of all. Great Britain and Sweden were locked together at 46 points each. Quite simply, whoever finished ahead of the other in heat twenty-five would be world champions. The enormous responsibility rested with two men.

In the red, white and blue corner was Scott Nicholls, the tenacious GB skipper who had accumulated six points including the bizarre incident where he retired from heat eighteen. Meanwhile in the yellow and blue corner stood Peter Karlsson who, after a fall first time out, had reeled off three impressive wins. Left on the sidelines when the British League clubs assembled their line-ups at the start of the season, the thirty-four-year-old Swede certainly had a point to prove. Also in the final race were Denmark's Hans Andersen and Poland's Tomasz Gollob, but with both their nation's positions already decided, neither had much to race for.

The atmosphere was thick with tension as the riders rode out for the crunch heat. Naturally a huge ovation was reserved for Nicholls, the man who was to carry the home hopes. All eyes were on Nicholls on gate one and Karlsson on the outside, but it was Andersen who was first away from gate three. The other three jostled for position around the first turn and, as they reached the back straight, the Brit was pinned on the kerb by Andersen as Karlsson flashed past on the outside. On the next bend Nicholls swept around Andersen, but already Karlsson was pulling clear. In the ensuing three laps, the Brit poured everything into the chase, but the harder he tried the further he fell back. Karlsson raised his hand as he crossed the line to mark victory for Sweden.

But for the Brits, it was hard to take. Nicholls rued his lost point from earlier in the evening. But he also pointed an accusing finger at Andersen – ironically his teammate at Ipswich – whom he felt had balked him in the final race, while allowing Karlsson to speed past. He said: 'I was the only rider to see the red light in heat eighteen and I guess I should have kept going. But in hindsight, that one point looks to have cost us the title. I am sure the person in the crowd didn't know what they were doing, but it was so disappointing. Heat twenty-five was a bitter pill to swallow. We had all ridden so hard, and with all our hearts, and everyone had given 110 per cent. Gate one wasn't working that well, but I made a good start and then for Hans to shut off and let Peter through made me very angry. I don't like to win or lose like that and it is not something I would ever do. You are out there to race, and I am not saying Sweden didn't deserve to win, but that is not the way to win.'

Controversial stuff. But TV replays seem to reinforce Nicholls' contention. The Dane twice looked at Karlsson on the straight before apparently twisting his right wrist forward to indicate he was throttling off. The Dane defended himself vehemently, saying: 'I've a totally clear conscience. I don't have sleepless nights or anything because I know I didn't do anything to let Sweden win. I have a totally 110 per cent clear conscience. I didn't agree anything with the Swedish team manager to help them win it before I went out. It's down to riders themselves to decide whether one country should win or not win – everything should be settled on the track. I think all this controversy is a bit unfair. I reckon the best thing I could have done was just go into the tapes. People are moaning and shouting but they have never sat on a bike or anything before. If they had ridden, they would know you go down the straight and if you are spinning and wind the throttle on, you spin even more. People threatened me and everything after the meeting. I didn't get anything out of Sweden winning in front of England.'

It was an incident that certainly left one or two riders with steam coming out of the helmets. But not so Peter Karlsson. The unassuming Swede was the coolest man in the stadium. He said: 'I felt I was under no pressure going into the last race. It's strange, but that was how I felt. I treated it just like a normal race. I just concentrated on getting a good gate. I was a little bit behind Scotty going into the first corner but I did a good first turn and edged ahead of him. I had the speed away from there. I was willing the bike to stay together in one piece and make the four laps. It was an excellent night and a great meeting.'

The controversial last heat.

7 August 2004: Poole: World Cup Final

SWEDEN

		1	2	3	4	5	6	Total
1	Mikael Max	2	1	3	1	2	–	9
2	Tony Rickardsson	3	3	3	0	3	–	12
3	Antonio Lindback	1	3	0	3	2	–	9
4	Andreas Jonsson	1	1	2	0	3	–	7
5	Peter Karlsson	EX	3	3	3	3	–	12

GREAT BRITAIN

		1	2	3	4	5	6	Total
1	David Norris	1	3	3	1	1	–	9
2	Lee Richardson	1	0	3	3	3	–	10
3	Mark Loram	3	2	2	3	2	–	12
4	Scott Nicholls	3	1	2	RET.	2	–	8
5	Gary Havelock	3	1	2	2	1	–	9

DENMARK

		1	2	3	4	5	6	Total
1	Hans Andersen	3	2	1	2	3	0	11
2	Nicki Pedersen	0	2	1	1	EX	–	4
3	Kenneth Bjerre	2	1	1	0	–	–	4
4	Niels-Kristian Iversen	F	3	1	0	1	–	5
5	Bjarne Pedersen	1	2	2	2	1	–	8

POLAND

		1	2	3	4	5	6	Total
1	Krzysztof Kasprzak	0	0	0	–	–	–	0
2	Jarek Hampel	2	0	0	2	0	–	4
3	Tomasz Gollob	0	F	0	0	1	–	1
4	Janusz Kolodziej	2	2	2	1	3	EX	10
5	Marcin Rempala	2	0	0	2	1	2	7

Heat 1 (rerun): Andersen, Max, Norris, Kasprzak, 60.11 secs

Heat 2: Rickardsson, Hampel, Richardson, N.Pedersen, 59.54 secs

Heat 3: Loram, Bjerre, Lindback, Gollob, 59.76 secs

Heat 4: Nicholls, Kolodziej, Jonsson, Iversen (F), 60.63 secs

Heat 5 (rerun): Havelock, Rempala, B.Pedersen, Karlsson (EX), 60.64 secs

Heat 6: Iversen, Loram, Max, Rempala, 59.90 secs

Heat 7 (rerun): Rickardsson, B.Pedersen, Nicholls, Kasprzak, 59.93 secs

Heat 8: Lindback, Andersen, Havelock, Hampel, 60.15 secs

Heat 9 (rerun): Norris, N.Pedersen, Jonsson, Gollob (F), 61.61 secs

Heat 10 (rerun): Karlsson, Kolodziej, Bjerre, Richardson, 60.57 secs

Heat 11: Max, Nicholls, Bjerre, Hampel, 60.14 secs

Heat 12: Rickardsson, Havelock, Iversen, Gollob, 59.93 secs

Heat 13 (rerun): Norris, Kolodziej, B.Pedersen, Lindback, 60.24 secs

Heat 14: Richardson, Jonsson, Andersen, Rempala, 60.34 secs

Heat 15: Karlsson, Loram, N.Pedersen, Kasprzak, 60.36 secs

Heat 16: Richardson, B.Pedersen, Max, Gollob, 59.29 secs

Heat 17: Loram, Andersen, Kolodziej, Rickardsson, 59.84 secs

Heat 18: Lindback, Rempala, N.Pedersen, Nicholls (RET.), 60.22 secs

Heat 19: Andersen, Havelock, Rempala, Jonsson, 60.80 secs

Heat 20: Karlsson, Hampel, Norris, Iversen, 60.43 secs

Heat 21 (rerun): Kolodziej, Max, Havelock, N.Pedersen (EX), 63.20 secs

Heat 22: Rickardsson, Rempala, Norris, Bjerre, 59.70 secs

Heat 23 (rerun): Richardson, Lindback, Iversen, Kolodziej (EX), 60.47 secs

Heat 24: Jonsson, Loram, B.Pedersen, Hampel, 60.90 secs

Heat 25: Karlsson, Nicholls, Gollob, Andersen, 60.39 secs

Other titles published by Tempus

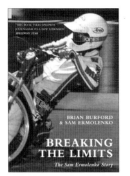

Breaking the Limits The Sam Ermolenko Story
BRIAN BURFORD & SAM ERMOLENKO

After a horrific road accident in his native California left him virtually
unable to walk, it took Sam Ermolenko an awful lot of bravery and
determination to make a recovery – let alone become a speedway World
Champion! Despite a late start in the sport and a further series of severe
injuries, Sam has overcome all the odds and reached the very top. This is his
remarkable story.
0 7524 3225 7

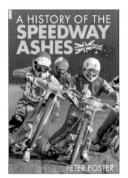

A History of the Speedway Ashes
PETER FOSTER

Between the wars, tens of thousands of spectators would turn up to see
Aussie greats like Vic Huxley, Lionel Van Praag and Bluey Wilkinson take on
the best English riders as the two nations contested speedway's 'Ashes'. One
of the biggest events in world speedway for many years, even in recent times
these series have been contested by some of the greatest riders in the sport.
This illustrated volume relives the glory days of the speedway ashes and will
be a superb read for anyone interested in the history of the sport.
0 7524 3468 3

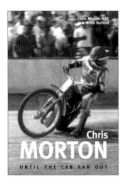

Chris Morton Until the Can Ran Out
CHRIS MORTON MBE & BRIAN BURFORD

Chris Morton is regarded as one of Britain's greatest ever speedway riders as
he won almost every honour that was open to him. A talented racer, he was
respected by his rivals and was one of the most exciting riders of his
generation. *Until the Can Ran Out* takes the reader on an enthralling journey
to the highest level of the sport – a ruthless place where all that matters is to
be a winner.
0 7524 3473 X

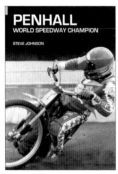

Penhall World Speedway Champion
STEVE JOHNSON

In less than five years, Bruce Penhall, the blond-haired, blue-eyed golden boy
of America, had gone from British League novice to World Speedway
Champion and was hailed as arguably the most popular champion there has
ever been. Overcoming personal tragedy at eighteen to become World
Champion again in high-speed powerboat racing and subsequently a
Hollywood movie star, the story of the charismatic Bruce Lee Penhall is an
exhilarating read for every speedway fan.
0 7524 3400 4

If you are interested in purchasing other books published by Tempus, or in case you have difficulty finding any
Tempus books in your local bookshop, you can also place orders directly through our website
www.tempus-publishing.com